THE PHANTOM HAND
And Other American Hauntings

THE PHANTOM HAND AND OTHER AMERICAN HAUNTINGS

by
Walter Harter

illustrated by
Robert Totten

Prentice-Hall, Inc., Englewood Cliffs, N.J.

Printed in the United States of America   • J

Prentice-Hall International, Inc., London
Prentice-Hall of Australia, Pty. Ltd., North
Sydney
Prentice-Hall of Canada, Ltd., Toronto
Prentice-Hall of India Private Ltd., New Delhi
Prentice-Hall of Japan, Inc., Tokyo

Library of Congress Cataloging in Publication Data

Harter, Walter L
    The phantom hand, and other American
hauntings.
    SUMMARY: Traces the background of sev-
eral purported cases of ghosts and other hauntings from all periods of United States history.
    1. Ghosts—United States—Juvenile literature.
[1. Ghosts] I. Totten, Robert. II. Title.
BF1472.U6H37   133.1'29'73   75–35955
ISBN 0-13-661843-X; 0-13-661819-7 (pbk.)
10   9   8   7   6   5   4   3   2

*To Edna—who still believes in those things
that make strange noises in the night.*

TABLE OF CONTENTS

THE PHANTOM HAND
And Other American Hauntings

PREFACE

There are many homes and buildings that have witnessed events of great importance to the history of our country. Some of them are still standing. Some have disappeared. Many of them are haunted, not only by the people who took part in those momentous happenings, but some of the houses and buildings themselves seem to have ghostly spirits of their own.

Some of those houses and buildings are so famous that everyone knows them. Independence Hall, in Philadelphia where the Declaration of Independence was adopted, is one. Faneuil Hall, in Boston, is another. There patriots gathered to plan ways of obtaining their liberty from England. It is rightfully called "The Cradle of Freedom." One more house, of the famous ones, would be the McLean Home at Appomattox, Virginia, where General Lee surrendered to General Grant, ending the Civil War that threatened to tear our country apart.

These very famous buildings, and others, are like large pieces of a mosaic. They form the principal parts of the picture of our independence. But there are smaller parts, too, just as important, because without them the complete picture might not have been possible. The stories in this book are about some of those little-known parts of the mosaic, the small pieces of the giant jig-saw that make the picture of our country complete.

Not all the people who contributed to our history were generals, politicians, or fighting men. There were some who played their parts accidentally, like James Marshall who found the gold that made our country rich, or Mary McCleod Bethune, the dedicated black woman, whose dream of a college for Negroes became reality.

There were also many writers and artists who helped form the cultural background of the United States. Henry Wadsworth Longfellow, one of our poets, certainly added a colorful piece to the final sparkling picture.

And not all the buildings that were the scenes of these small, but important, events, were imposing or grand. The mission and fort called The Alamo is not as beautiful as Independence Hall, but what happened at those adobe walls won freedom for one third of our nation's area. The wooden shed in Kansas, where exhausted men and ponies rested during their swift journeys to the shores of the Pacific Ocean, has little of the splendor of Fanueil Hall. But that old building, and dozens like it, was the beginning of a communication system that drew together the far parts of our country.

The small prison in a town in the coal regions of Pennsyvania can't compare with the pomp and ceremony of the surrender of armies in Virginia, but because of that drab building, one of our great unions was born, assuring our nation of the energy that built and is still building most of our civilization.

The ghosts that haunt these places aren't all as sad and tragic as the apparition of Longfellow, who wanders through the rooms of Craigie House, or the men who were massacred while defending The Alamo, or even the man who, minutes before he was hanged, placed his handprint on the wall of "Cell Number Eight," in the prison at Mauch Chunk, Pennsylvania, a handprint that has returned, even after the wall was torn down and rebuilt.

There are also many happy ghosts in these small pieces of the jig-saw, like the specters of the children and the jolly, stout man who frolic on the lawns of Sagamore Hill, or the phantom who stays in the small cottage at Monticello, the home of the man who wrote the Declaration of Independence.

And there are apparitions of other things, too. Buildings that have disappeared long ago—like the Armory and Arsenal at Harper's Ferry—often are seen by people, exactly as they were many years before.

The phantoms of animals often appear, not only pets, but other creatures, too, like the foam-flecked horses of the Pony Express as they pass weary car-drivers on the four-lane highway that once was the Oregon-California Trail.

Some tourists who have visited the Colosseum at Rome say they saw and heard not only the crowds that came to watch the cruel events that were enacted there, but also the animals that took part in them—lions fighting tigers and elephants battling for their lives against packs of wild dogs and wolves.

Sometimes, too, men who have taken part in a fierce battle of one of our wars stand in the quietness of those fields and witness that battle again. They hear the shouts and cries of the men and even see the flashes of the guns.

But these are *sensitive* people. They are said to be *psychic*, aware of forces beyond our physical world. They often see, hear, and even feel what others are completely unaware of. We all have that ability to some degree, because all of us at some time have *sensed* the unknown, the unexplainable.

But how is it possible that the apparitions of people, animals, and even things can be seen? This is one possible explanation: There is a theory that *nothing in our world is lost*. Things might disappear in the forms as we know them, but what they are composed of, their atoms, are still in the atmosphere.

A building burns. But is it really destroyed? We can't see it now as it was, but are the atoms it was made of still in the air? And if a person dies, are the molecules that composed the body floating in the atmosphere?

The very small parts of all things that once had shape and form might be *reassembled* by the eyes and in the minds of some people who are more sensitive than others to things outside the physical world. It might be as if they could slip on a pair of special spectacles when they look at a jumbled jig-saw puzzle and instantly the completed picture is brought together in their minds.

This is just an idea, a suggestion, but it might explain, in a very simple way, how people and things that once *were*, can be seen again by those who have a special gift.

There are some things we use every day, and have become accustomed to, that are just as strange. In radio and television, for instance, pictures and sounds are put into the air, then reassembled by catching their vibrations, rays, or atoms on a slim wire thousands of miles away.

Perhaps people who are psychic are walking antennas, who can catch and put together again shapes and forms that apparently have disappeared.

Anyway, there *are* ghosts and there *are* people who see them.

THE
GHOSTLY POET
OF CRAIGIE HOUSE

One sunny day in August 1837 a tall man knocked on the door of a large house on Brattle Street, Cambridge, Massachusetts. It was called Craigie House. It had a history of happiness as well as tragedy. More evil would come to those who would live in it.

Andrew Craigie, a general in the Revolutionary Army, had remodeled the ancient mansion for his young bride, less than half his age. But after he died, his fortune had passed away too. Hard times had come to the house on Brattle Street. Now the elderly Mrs. Craigie, only a pale imitation of the young girl who had come there to live, was forced to rent rooms to some of the students who studied at the nearby Harvard College.

If the young man could have foretold the tragedy that would happen to him in that house, perhaps he might have turned and run down that lovely tree-lined street. Instead he knocked again on the broad door.

When it was eventually opened by a frail old lady, the young man asked if he could rent a few rooms. But it was a hot day and Mrs. Craigie was out of patience with some of the students who lived with her, so she curtly answered "No." Besides the only rooms available were two of the best ones. They had been lived in by General George Washington and Mrs. Washington when the house was headquarters for the American Army, more than sixty years before, and were rented to only very special guests.

The young man, disappointed, was about to leave when he noticed a small book lying on the hall table. The title was *Outre-Mer* (Beyond the Sea). It was a series of short essays he had written describing his journey through Europe.

"Did you like my book?" he asked Mrs. Craigie and pointed to the name of the author beneath the strange title—Henry Wadsworth Longfellow.

Mrs. Craigie was impressed and even more so when Mr. Longfellow told her he wasn't a student but the new professor of modern languages at Harvard. She rented him the two rooms.

Although he was then just thirty years of age, he had already experienced one of life's greatest tragedies. When he was twenty-four years old he had married Mary Storer Porter, his childhood sweetheart. Three years later, in 1834, he received leave of absence from Bowdoin College, where he was teaching English, to go abroad to study modern languages.

The young couple had had two wonderful years in Europe. They spent many hours each day in the great libraries of famous cities. They also rented rooms in modest homes of every country they visited and learned to speak the different languages. Then their perfect world exploded.

It was while they were living and studying in Rotterdam, Holland, in 1835, that a deadly fever swept through Europe, and his young bride died in his arms.

The young poet was brokenhearted. He and his wife had worked together so closely and had so many common interests that he was sure he couldn't face life without her. For weeks after he sent her small body back to America he kept to his room, going out only at night to stroll along the canals and think. Finally he decided that he couldn't continue to live and work in this world alone.

Late one night he tried to kill himself. He climbed to the top of one of the bridges that spanned a wide canal and leaped into the water. But two young friends who had been trying to console him in his grief and had followed him that night, pulled him safely to the bank. Those friends also sent his essays to an American publisher.

It was as if that leap into the water restored Longfellow's sanity. Several months later he packed his few belongings and went to Switzerland. He took lodgings with a local family and began to study the language. It was there that he saw for the first time the girl who would become the second and greatest tragedy of his life.

Her name was Frances Appleton. She was from Boston. She and her wealthy family were making a leisurely tour of Europe. Longfellow met the young lady twice, but those two brief encounters were enough. He fell desperately in love with her and vowed that—no matter how long it would take—he would eventually marry her.

And it did take a long time—seven years.

Frances Appleton had been pleasant and kind to Longfellow during their two short meetings. She felt sorry for the tragedy that had marred his life. But to her he was just another young American traveling on the continent. Even after they both were back in America and Longfellow called at the Appleton mansion in Boston, she was kind and pleasant but no more.

It was then that Longfellow wrote his only novel. It is a love story which concerns a young American poet traveling in Europe who meets an American girl and falls in love with her. They meet frequently, in the story, and he tries in various ways to get her to return his love. But the girl doesn't take his courtship seriously. The tale ends sadly when the girl returns to America and the desolated poet continues his lonely wandering.

Everyone who knew the young couple understood that the story was a true one. The young poet was Longfellow, and the girl who wouldn't return his love was Frances Appleton. Longfellow even sent Frances a tenderly inscribed copy of the book. But she didn't reply. And, one day when they happened to pass each other on a Boston street, she ignored his lifted hat. At the end of that day Longfellow wrote in his journal, "It is ended."

But it didn't end there. Longfellow continued to send the girl flowers and pieces of poetry. And if he could possibly manage it, he attended every party or gathering where he thought he might meet her. He became obsessed with the desire to win and wed her.

Finally, little by little, she began to return his interest. He saw her more often and even was invited to have dinner at the Appleton home. At last, seven years after seeing her for the first time, she agreed to marry him. As a wedding gift Nathan Appleton bought the young couple the Craigie House. It was remodeled, refurnished, and the Harvard students had to find lodgings elsewhere.

Longfellow's marriage to the girl he so passionately loved seemed to open the dam of genius that was in his heart and mind. One after another great poems gushed from his pen: "The Wreck of the Hesperus," "The Village Blacksmith," "Evangeline," "The Song of Hiawatha," "The Courtship of Miles Standish," and dozens more.

At the top of the Craigie House in one of the rooms that had been occupied by General Washington, Longfellow made a study. It was there in the evenings, with Frances sitting by the fireside doing the elaborate embroidery that was her hobby, that he would pace up and down, reading the lines he had composed that day.

"She seems to know when things *sound* right," he wrote in his journal.

Poetry began to take up so much of Longfellow's time that in 1854 he resigned his professorship so that nothing would interfere with his writing.

It was an ideal relationship between the poet and the girl he loved so deeply. She was kept busy running the house and directing the servants. He took long walks into the countryside and through the city streets, composing the lines he would put on paper later in the day.

But the nights were special. When the children were abed (they had five during the years), when the house became silent, they would be together in the cozy study at the top of the house. The tall man would pace back and forth, reciting the lines he had created, while his wife listened, either nodding approval or making quiet suggestions. There was happiness and contentment at last in the Craigie House.

But sometimes the fates attack those who are the most happy and contented.

It was a warm July night in 1861. All the windows were open in the study. Longfellow had just gone to his desk to make some corrections on a manuscipt. Frances had put aside her embroidery hoop and was sealing some locks of their childrens' hair in little boxes—when the furies struck.

She had turned to reach for some ribbon when her arm knocked over a lighted candle. It fell onto the gauzy summer dress she was wearing. In a few seconds she was covered in leaping flames that were fanned into an inferno by the breeze from the open windows.

Longfellow ran to her, threw his arms around her and tried to beat out the waves of fire, but he couldn't save her. She was dead when the servants ran into the room in answer to his cries for help. Longfellow himself was so badly burned he was unable to attend her funeral three days later.

He never wrote another famous poem. It was as though the genius of his heart and mind had died in the blaze that consumed his loved one.

Henry Wadsworth Longfellow lived to be an old man. He died in 1881 at the age of 77. His fame had spread to every part of the world. His poems were read in every language. Famous men and women came from far places to visit with the man who had composed lines of verse that would live as long as there is a written language. The children married and became involved in lives of their own. The poet was alone in the Craigie House.

There is a bright plaque on that house today. Visitors wander through the rooms, and some, if they're lucky and know about it, can peek into the cozy study at the top of the house.

But visitors leave and the house becomes silent at night. There are those who live on that street who say that lights burn in the windows of that room at the top of the house. There are even some who say they often see a tall shadow pacing back and forth across those lighted windows. But they are the very sensitive ones.

THE GHOSTS
WHO GO TO COLLEGE

Seventy years ago tourists on the streets of Daytona Beach, Florida, stared in astonishment at a huge black woman riding a bicycle. Balanced on the handlebars was a large basket filled with sweet-potato pies.

At every street corner the woman would stop her battered bicycle, gather the passersby, and try to sell the still warm pastries.

She was Mrs. Mary McLeod Bethune, and she was trying to make come true a dream that had been singing in her heart. It was to teach young black boys and girls how to read and write.

The money she earned by baking and selling sweet-potato pies paid the rent for a shack on the city dump and bought pads of writing paper. For pens her students used charred sticks and the juice of berries.

Mrs. Mary McLeod Bethune was the fifteenth child of slave parents. Born in 1875 in South Carolina, she helped her parents work the few acres of land they had saved for and bought after the Civil War.

As a child Mary McLeod had one driving ambition. She wanted to read the Bible. Each night her prayers ended with the plea, "Dear God please let me learn to read."

Her prayers were answered one day when a Negro missionary started a small school in a church not far from the McLeod's cabin. The missionary called on the black families in the area, pleading that one child from each home be sent to the school. The plan was that each chosen child would teach the others in the family.

When her father looked over his brood of fifteen something in Mary's eager face made him select her. "I believe she'll be able to teach all of us," he said, "and besides she's too young to work very hard."

The little black girl trudged five miles to school each day and five miles back home. She studied hard, and at night around the kitchen table by the light of home-made candles, she taught her brothers, sisters, father, and mother to read and write.

Her proudest moment came when, as the brightest student in the small school, she was given a Bible as a prize. That night, when she showed the Bible to her family, it accidentally opened up to John 3:16. "For God so loved the world that He gave His only begotten son, so that whosoever believeth in Him shall not perish but have everlasting life".

To Mary McLeod's eyes the word "whosoever" lay on the page like a flame. It meant *everyone*, not just whites. It meant blacks too. All people were equal in the sight of God.

From that moment on her life was dedicated to acquiring an education, not only for herself, but so she could pass it on to others of her race.

The black girl's determination amazed her teachers.

She studied every free moment. But there was also work to do on the small farm. Often she joined her brothers and sisters in pulling the plow when their old mule died.

After that first school closed, the teachers remembered Mary McLeod, and finally she received a scholarship to Scotia Seminary in Concord, North Carolina. This was followed by another scholarship to the Moody Institute in Chicago, where she majored in religion.

In 1898 when she was twenty-three years old and teaching in Sumpter, South Carolina, she met and married another teacher, Albert Bethune. They saved their money and a few years later opened a small school in Palatka, northern Florida. A few months after it opened the school burned down, and Mr. Bethune died of a heart attack. Many people believed that the Ku Klux Klan had destroyed the school, but there was no proof.

At that time a railroad was being built along Florida's east coast, using black laborers, who were housed at the headquarters in Daytona Beach. When Mrs. Bethune heard of the dreadful living conditions of those workers, she immediately went there and tried to open a school so the black children could learn to read and write.

It was a difficult task. The Ku Klux Klan was active in that area, and the Negro families were afraid to help the big black woman with her dream of Negro education. But she kept trying, and finally she found an abandoned shack on the edge of the city dump.

"The owner wanted $11 a month rent," she wrote later, "and I had only $1.50. I pleaded with him for hours. He finally consented to take the $1.50 and trust me for the rest."

She begged at stores for flour, shortening and sweet-potatoes to bake the pies she sold from door to door from her battered bicycle. "In a week I had enough money for the rent." Then she prowled over the dump, looking for things she could mend for use in the school or to sell.

At last on October 3, 1904 her school opened. She called it the Daytona Educational and Industrial School for Negro Girls. She was the only teacher. There were five pupils, girls whose families defied the Ku Klux Klan and agreed to pay a tuition of fifty cents a week. The desks were packing boxes. The pencils were charred sticks dipped in berry juice.

Of course on that great day she didn't forget Him who was responsible. Her deep contralto led the treble voices in the hymn, "Leaning on the Everlasting Arms." Then she recited "The Lord is my shepherd, I shall not want . . ." and classes began.

The school taught reading, writing, cooking, and sewing, because Mrs. Bethune realized that black girls would have difficulty entering the business world. That would come much later. It was enough now to teach them how to earn a living.

Mrs. Bethune taught her small girls to sing in harmony, then took them around to the grand hotels in the area. They sang in the lobbies of the hotels and in the streets and took up collections.

She watched the society columns of the newspapers, and when millionaires from the North came to Daytona, she would arrange for her small group to sing for them. John D. Rockefeller not only gave the children shiny dimes, but many years later after his death, his family donated an organ to the school. Thomas H. White, of the White Sewing Machine Company, wandered into the tiny school one day and placed on Mrs. Bethune's desk all the money he had in his pockets. When he died he left enough money to build White Hall, now the main assembly building.

More and more black girls came to the school. Soon there were 250 of them, and all were taught and fed. But a larger building was badly needed. Although the Ku Klux Klan had ceased to openly bother Mrs. Bethune, the whites in the area still refused to help her build another school.

Finally she bought the city dump. The owner demanded $200 for the land. Again she pleaded and argued, and at last he agreed to take $5 down and the remainder in two years. That meant more and more pies to be baked and sold and more singing by the groups she had taught. Some small donations trickled in but not nearly enough to build a school.

She went to every contractor, begging for building materials. From the dump she and the children salvaged broken bricks and pieces of wood. For labor she traded tuitions to fathers for their children. The men worked on the structure in the evenings and on their days off.

She named the finished building Faith Hall, because hope, labor—and faith—had made it possible.

It wasn't much of a building, only four walls and a roof. The ground floor was of dirt. The second floor was pieces of old wood nailed together. The rooms had movable walls made from matting the girls found on the dump.

In the daytime the rooms were used for classes. At night they became places to sleep for the fifty or so girls from outlying places who couldn't return home at night. There was a large kitchen, because hundreds of mouths had to be fed each day, and the sweet-potato pies still had to be baked and sold.

She had a little trouble with the white plumbers who installed some of the pipes. At first they refused to put in the three bathrooms she wanted. They were sure, they said, that Negroes would never be able to learn how to use them. But she was used to arguing now, and the bathrooms went in.

Then the Ku Klux Klan struck.

At first they had left her alone, thinking the project would fail, but when Faith Hall became a reality they were determined to ruin it. One night Mrs. Bethune was warned that the Klan would attack Faith Hall.

She and the girls tried to sleep, but soon after midnight they were aroused by the blasts of many horns. When they looked outside they saw that hundreds of men in white hoods had surrounded the small building. Most of the men were on horseback. Their frightened animals pawed the ground and neighed shrilly at the sound of the trumpets that blared into the night.

While Mrs. Bethune and the frightened girls watched, some of the hooded men erected a large cross in front of the house and set it on fire. Other men carrying buckets of kerosene began to creep toward the building.

Suddenly a powerful voice began to sing the hymn— "Be not dismayed, What'er Betide, God Will Take Care of You—" Slowly the voices of the girls joined in. One after another the grand old hymns rang out into the night.

For a long time the hooded men sat on their horses in the flickering light of the blazing torch. Then lightning flashed among the tall oaks and palms and it began to rain. Slowly, quietly the hooded men turned their horses and rode away.

"We sang them right off the campus!" Mrs. Bethune told friends later, "But God sent the rain."

The college did succeed. In 1923 it absorbed the Cookman Institute of Jacksonville and became Bethune-Cookman, one of the oldest and most respected of Black coeducational colleges.

The huge black woman became a friend of the great and influential. Five Presidents including Theodore Roosevelt, Coolidge, Hoover, Truman, and Franklin Roosevelt named her advisor in Negro affairs and called her to the White House from time to time. Mrs. Bethune died in 1955 at the age of 80.

New students are, of course, told the story of that first tiny building and of the night when the girls' voices, led by Mrs. Bethune's strong contralto, "sang the hooded men right off the campus."

Over the years many of the students have claimed that on stormy nights when lightning flashes through the oaks and palms and lights up the small building, they see a blazing cross. Some are also sure they can hear the sound of girls singing hymns, led by one strong, deep voice.

Perhaps they do.

THE
PHANTOM HAND PRINT
IN CELL NUMBER
EIGHT

There is the print of a man's hand on the wall of cell number eight in the prison of the small town of Mauch Chunk in southeastern Pennsylvania. For nearly 100 years that ghostly print has returned, no matter how often the wall has been replaced or replastered. The man who placed it there was accused of taking part in a series of horrible events that changed one of the great industries of the United States.

The story of that haunted hand began on a warm June morning in 1878. Early on that bright day four men in new black suits walked slowly to where a gallows had been erected in the corridor of the prison in that town that was the center of the anthracite, or "hard coal," mines.

Each man carried a single red rose in his calloused hand. They wore black hoods over their heads, and thick ropes were tightened around their necks. At a signal from a prison official a lever was pulled, and the four men dropped through four trap doors. They were hanged by their necks until they were dead.

Forty miles away in another small town, Pottsville,

six other men were hanged that day. Within a few months ten more men swung at the ends of ropes until they were dead. All these men were Irish and of a band of criminals called the Molly Maguires. They had been found guilty of hundreds of murders, burnings, and explosions. They had murdered mine owners and foremen and burned or exploded many of the coal mines in southeastern Pennsylvania.

The Molly Maguires, what they did, and what happened to them resulted in the formation of one of the most powerful unions in our country—The United Mine Workers of America.

That union is still powerful today. Its members control the production of our greatest natural resource—coal—which due to the energy crisis that faces our country today and will continue to be a problem in the future is now more important than ever. But "hard coal," or anthracite, was just as important a hundred years ago. We were entering the Industrial Revolution, and factories, ships, and railroads demanded more and more fuel to create energy. Anthracite coal burned longer and created more energy than any other kind. And most of our country's supply of that "black gold" lay deep in the earth in southeastern Pennsylvania.

What really started the series of events that ended in the prison at Mauch Chunk began more than thirty years before, 3000 miles across the sea, in Ireland.

For many generations the lives of the Irish people depended on potatoes. They grew, exported, and ate them. Potatoes were their lives.

Then in three sad years between 1845 and 1847, a

blight, or sickness, struck the fields, and there were no more potatoes. Irishmen lost their farms and homes, and many of them starved to death. Irish families left their homeland by the thousands, and most of them came to the land of their dreams—America.

For many of them that dream became a nightmare. Most of those immigrants were farmers; many were unschooled and fit for only the lowest kinds of labor. But there was work for them, work that most Americans refused to do. That was to go deep into the bowels of the earth and dig up the black rocks that burned—coal.

The anthracite mines always needed workers, because not only was the labor exhausting, but breathing the black dust and daily accidents deep in the earth cost many lives, so new workers had to be found constantly. Even the tide of unfortunate immigrants wasn't enough, and salesmen were sent to Ireland to sell the "dream" of America. Irishmen were promised high wages, lovely homes, and schools for their children.

Many thousands believed that dream. They came to the United States, their fares paid, ready for the promised opportunity in this new country where all were equal. What they found were "shanty" towns, no schools, and little pay. They became the slaves of the mine owners. The shacks they lived in were owned by the mines, and the only stores where they could buy food and clothing were operated by the mine owners.

The average pay of a miner was four dollars a week, but he was never paid that amount. After sums were deducted for the rent of the shack he and his family lived in (usually one room with a dirt floor) and for the food he bought at the company's store, he was lucky if he had ten cents left. Most of the Irish miners saw no money at all. They were always in debt to the mine owners for rent, food, and clothing. And these "debts" were passed on to the sons when their fathers died.

These sons usually began to work in the mines at the age of five or six as "breaker boys." Their job was to sit astride shutes, down which flowed streams of coal, and to pick out slate and stones from the "black gold." Their hands became like black claws. And when they reached the age of twelve they took their places in the mines, digging, and breathing the black dust from dawn until dusk.

It was a sad time. The miners couldn't leave their jobs because of the debts they owed the company. If they tried to run away they were arrested and put in jail until they promised to go back to the "pits." There were no laws to protect them. There were no safety rules. The flimsy shafts that sank ever deeper into the earth collapsed again and again, burying miners whose bodies were never recovered. But there were always new immigrants to take their places.

Wherever miners gathered, in one another's shacks or under the dim yellow glow of gas lights on street corners, they talked of ways to improve their lives and the lives of their families. Some of them had heard of organizations called "unions," through which workers in other industries had banded together to present a united front to the owners of factories. But most of them had been failures. Only the small unions in the railroad and steel industries had been partially successful.

But it was worth a try. The first "strike" called by the coal miners took place in 1847 in Schuylkill County, Pennsylvania. It was a dismal failure. The mine owners imported armed thugs from New York and Philadelphia to "break" the strike. The result was that many miners were killed and many more were beaten.

Those miners whose names were known were fined, and that fine was added to the debts they owed the companies. They were also placed on a blacklist and were watched by detectives and policemen as "trouble makers." When new immigrants were available, those on the blacklist lost their jobs, but their debts weren't forgiven. They were hounded, some for the rest of their lives, no matter where they went.

And so the Molly Maguires was formed. It was a secret society, dedicated to right their wrongs by violence, and to try to force the mine owners to treat them as human beings.

Although there are many legends about how that name was selected, the most reliable is that it was the name of an Irish widow who, with her five children, was put out of her home in Dublin by British landowners and had to beg in the streets.

The Irishmen who belonged to the "Mollies" were carefully chosen. They took a solemn oath of allegiance to the society and to one another. Every member was watched carefully by the others, and if there was the slightest suspicion that a Molly was a spy for the owners, he was killed or horribly tortured as an example.

A Mauch Chunk newspaper reported that on a spring morning in 1866 a man was walking oddly down the main street of the town. His face was bloody, and the black hole that was his mouth greedily gulped the nippy air. His tongue had been cut out. His arms hung strangely from his shoulders because both had been broken in several places. His name was Jim Sweeny. He wasn't a Molly, but he had carried information about the secret society to the mine owners, in exchange for a better house for his family.

The Molly Maguires comprised only a small percentage of all the miners. Most of the workers were not violent men. They wanted improvement in their lives, but they knew that killings and burnings would not help them. Although they knew who the Mollies were, they kept silent. What happened to Jim Sweeny and other informers was an example to those who were not members of the society. So those who lived in the shanty towns kept silent. They saw nothing. They told nothing. They lived in fear of both the Mollies and the mine owners.

The Molly Maguires became more violent. Mine owners and foremen were shot dead when they answered a knock on their doors, and their houses were burned down. Dynamite was exploded in many mines, making them useless. Some mine fires burned for more than twenty years, because the flames fed on the black rock that stretched for miles in wide seams beneath the earth.

The mine owners held a conference. Something had to be done to stop the violence and soon. But what?

The ringleaders of the Molly Maguires would have to be discovered, brought to trial, and executed. But how?

Finally the mine owners went to the Pinkerton Detective Agency in Chicago. Allan Pinkerton had been with the Chicago police force for twenty-five years. He also had been responsible for the creation of the United States' Secret Service. The motto of his detective agency was "The Eye that Never Sleeps." Pinkerton's advice was worth listening to.

"I know exactly the type of man you need," he told the mine owners. "He must be a special man, with a 'cover' that will be acceptable to the miners. It will take a little time, but I'll find the man you need."

It took almost a year, but the right man was found. His name was James McParlan. He had worked in the mines in Ireland and knew about mine owners and the terrible conditions under which miners worked and lived.

"I'm Irish," he told the mine owners at a meeting in Chicago, "and I know how badly the miners have been treated. I'm sure that sometime laws will be made to protect them. But I'm against violence. I've heard of some of the things the Mollies have done, and I'll do all I can to stop them."

It took McParlan almost four years to be accepted by the Molly Maguires. He changed his name to McKenna so that no one could trace his past. After working in various mines around Mauch Chunk and taking part in a few demonstrations, he was at last allowed to meet Jack Kehoe, the leader of the Mollies.

McParlan had played his part well. He had talked against the mine owners, and had even started a riot in one of the mines, and Jack Kehoe was sure McParlan would make a good member of the society.

The two men became friends at once. McKenna

(McParlan) had charm and courage, two things Jack Kehoe liked. At a ceremony one night in the cellar of Kehoe's house, McKenna signed his name in his own blood and became a member of the Mollies.

For two years McParlan was a Molly and did as he was orderd. He took part in burnings and explosions, and when at Molly meetings, a mine owner would be selected to be killed he would secretly let the authorities know so they could protect that man.

Bit by bit McParlan collected evidence against the Molly Maguires. His testimony in the courtroom of Mauch Chunk, county seat of Carbon County, in March 1878, sent the leaders of that dreaded secret society to their deaths by hanging.

The Molly Maguires did not start the union movement in the coal mines. They sought only to take revenge by violence. But the news of what they had done and why they did it made the public aware of the pitiful plight of the men who worked deep in the earth to supply energy for the growing industrial giants of the United States.

New unions were started, and peaceable men were proud to join them. In time those unions fought for and won the right to work in safety and earn a decent living, free from the dominance of the mine owners.

The small prison still stands on that street in Mauch Chunk. It has the usual number of ghosts, as all buildings do that have witnessed agony and death. But this building has one apparition that is stranger than most others.

It is the print of a hand.

One of the four Irishmen who were hanged that summer day in 1878 was named Thomas Fisher. From the start of the trial he had said he was not guilty, and even when the jailors came to take him to the gallows, he still shouted that he was innocent. As they were dragging him from his cell, he stopped and placed his hand high on the wall. "If I'm innocent that print will stay forever!" he cried as they pulled him away.

The perspiration mixed with the coal dust in his skin produced a black smudge on the white plaster. For nearly a hundred years that print of his hand has remained on the wall of cell number eight, even though over the years the wall has been torn down and replaced several times.

It is still there today.

People in the coal regions of southeastern Pennsylvania have never forgotten the legends of the Molly Maguires. Even now they say, with a quick glance over their shoulders, that very often at night—when the mists from the mines swirl around the yellow lights at street corners—they see shadowy figures and hear a song that was famous at that time:

"How far is it to Mauch Chunk, stranger, did you say?
"I guess it's about a dozen miles away,
"Straight out in that direction—over the hill.
"Do the Mollies still lie in wait to kill?"

THE
HAUNTED HOUSE
ON THE HILL

There is a strange house on top of a mountain near Charlottesville, Virginia. It is called Monticello. It was the home of Thomas Jefferson, third president of the United States and the author of the Declaration of Independence.

Some people call Monticello "The Haunted House on the Hill."

Late in the afternoon of January 18, 1772 a light snow began to fall. The tall, redheaded young man and the dark haired girl with him in the carriage thought it was an omen of good luck. They had been married only a few hours before and were on their way to a cottage the young man had built on top of a mountain.

The young man's name was Thomas Jefferson. He was twenty-nine years of age and already a member of Virginia's House of Burgesses. His bride was Martha Wayles Skelton.

The courtship had lasted for more than two years. Jefferson had ridden horseback each week to visit Martha at her family's plantation, called The Forest. And always behind him rode his boyhood companion,

Jupiter, a black man. Jupiter always had a violin strapped to his back, because Jefferson loved to play the instrument and took it with him wherever he went.

Martha had been willing to marry the young man earlier, but Jefferson had hesitated. His family home, Shadwell, had burned to the ground, and he was just beginning to practice as a lawyer.

But now he had entered politics, and more people were coming to his small office in Charlottesville to ask advice of the young lawyer who, many people said, was wise beyond his years. It was time to marry and raise a family.

Even before Shadwell had burned he had been making plans for a special house—a house he would design from the first brick to the last nail. This house would include many of the beautiful things he had seen in drawings of Roman and Greek homes, but it also would be American and would include all the inventions he had sketched in his notebooks.

It would have to be high on a hill so he could gaze over the lovely valleys of the Virginia he loved. Part of the land left to him by Peter Jefferson, his father, was called Monticello, which means "little mountain" in Italian. And that was the name he would give the house he would build there.

But first a great amount of work would have to be done. During the years before he married, workmen literally cut off the top of the mountain, so that there would be a plateau, or large flat space, on which to build. Then, realizing it would take years to erect the home he had planned, he built a small cottage on the site. It was there he and Martha would spend their honeymoon and live until the main structure was finished.

Snows are usually light in Virginia, just enough to spread a thin blanket of white over the roads. But occasionally a blizzard does strike. By early dusk the carriage was being dragged through drifts three feet high. Finally the straining horses could pull it no further.

They had passed plantations whose owners would have welcomed them and put them in warm beds until morning, but this was their wedding night, and they were determined to spend it in the cottage on top of Monticello.

They left the carriage in a ditch and mounted the horses. The breaths of the riders and their mounts hung in the bitterly cold air like streams of vapor when at last they reached the top of the mountain. Jefferson wanted Martha to go into the cottage at once, but she insisted on helping him bed down the animals in the flimsy shed that was attached to it.

The cottage was only one large room, but it had a huge fireplace in which Jefferson soon built a roaring fire. There, lying before the leaping flames, and drinking mugs of hot tea made from water boiled in an iron kettle that hung over the fire, Tom and Martha Jefferson began their strange honeymoon, which lasted almost a week, because it took that long for rescuers to dig their way up the winding road to the top of the mountain.

The Jeffersons never forgot that week. As the months passed the home Jefferson had planned slowly rose, room by room, and eventually they moved into a small part of it. But they kept the honeymoon cottage exactly as it was on that first night, and during the ten short years that Martha would live they went there often, sometimes spending entire nights and days.

As time passed Jefferson took an even more active part in the politics of Virginia and in the new country he and others were trying to carve out of a wilderness. In June 1775 when representatives of the thirteen colonies gathered in Philadelphia to issue a series of "Declarations" that set forth the rights of all the colonists, Thomas Jefferson was one of its youngest members.

And one year later in June 1776 when delegates decided to announce a "Declaration of Independence" with the stirring words, "We mutually pledge to each other our lives, our fortunes, and our sacred honor," it was Thomas Jefferson who wrote the first and last drafts of that important document.

But, busy as he was, the work on the home he called Monticello never stopped. Most of the materials used in building Monticello were made on the plateau. The stones for the foundation were dug from the side of the mountain. The bricks were made in a kiln on the site. Even the nails were made in a "nailery" on the property.

One of the things that made Monticello unique was the construction of two long terraces that stretched for hundreds of feet, one from the right and one from the left side of the house. At the end of the left terrace was the honeymoon cottage. At the end of the right terrace was a small building Jefferson used as his law office. Beneath the terraces were kitchens, stables, and storerooms.

As the years passed Martha gave birth to three daughters, and Jefferson became Governor of Virginia. They were happy years. The blizzard on their wedding night, which they had called a "good omen," seemed to be working.

But had it been a good omen? There were evil times ahead. Their marriage and the magnificent home they were building would eventually come crashing down. The first blow was Martha's death on September 6, 1782. She always had been frail, but no one, least of all Jefferson, expected her to die so young. On her death bed she begged Jefferson to promise never to remarry. She didn't want a strange woman bringing up her daughters.

Jefferson promised and kept his word. To keep his mind occupied he pressed on with the building of the house, sometimes staying with the workmen from dawn until dusk. He often changed plans and altered designs, but always the work progressed.

Then in 1784 he was sent to France as Minister of the new nation. He didn't want to go, but he finally agreed with the advice of his friends that a change of scene would ease the pain of Martha's death. He left explicit instructions for the further construction of Monticello, and the work went on.

He remained in Paris five years, taking care of the affairs of the new country he had helped create. When he had time he wandered through the shops of the city, selecting paintings, silverware, and ornaments to be sent back to Monticello. The house on the mountain was seldom from his thoughts.

When he returned to the United States in 1789, he

was determined to retire to Monticello, raise his daughters, and live "a gentle life with my memories."

But in 1790 President George Washington insisted that Jefferson become his secretary of state. He needed the mind of the man who had created the "Declaration of Independence."

For the next nineteen years Jefferson worked as hard to build the United States as he did to finish Monticello. Both of them were intertwined in his heart. Each had been started at the same time, and he wanted each of them to be as perfect and lasting as the mind of man could make them. The United States flourished as the best system of government ever devised. Monticello had the opposite fate.

During those nineteen years Jefferson became vice-president under our second president, John Adams. In 1801 he was elected the third president of the United States.

But still he spent every free moment at the home he loved, sometimes riding night and day to spend only a few hours at Monticello. The mansion was never completely finished, but it was, for many years, the most magnificent home in the United States.

But Monticello was not only a home. It was a monument to the creative genius of one man, because not only did Jefferson design everything in it from the windows to the drapes that covered them, but he invented hundreds of things that make the place fascinating, not only to those who knew it then but to the thousands who visit it now.

It had thirty-five rooms. In the huge entrance hall

was a seven-day clock worked by cannon balls which, as they slowly rose and fell, marked the days of the week. There were intricate dumbwaiters that brought food and wine from the kitchens beneath the terraces, and doors were cleverly designed so that as they turned, they brought food into the dining room from nearby warming places.

Jefferson never lost his love of music, so he built a stand that would hold the music for four musicians when they played the quartets he enjoyed. He built a revolving chair and table for his study which are still regarded as the work of an inventive genius.

The home looked like a jewel set in the greenery of the mountain top. Sunlight glistened from the dome that was cleverly constructed of thousands of small pieces of wood. On all sides of the house were gardens. There was even a pond where fresh fish were kept, ready to be taken to the kitchens.

The downfall of Monticello and the collapse of Jefferson's fortune were probably because of one great flaw in his character: he could not say "no" to anyone. Although he dreamed of retiring to Monticello, he accepted every position in the government that was offered to him. For in his mind the new country required as much attention and care as did his home. But that wasn't all. He couldn't say "no" to any friend who needed financial help. He loaned money at no interest, and he placed his name on notes for large sums, although he knew in his heart they would never be repaid.

He kept "open house" for all who stopped at the mansion on the mountain. Sometimes fifty people would be in the house at one time, all eating and drinking at his expense, and many of them staying for weeks. During many of these times Jefferson would slip away to the Honeymoon Cottage, often staying there for days, alone, writing and studying. His food would be brought to him by Jupiter, his still faithful servant and companion.

Jefferson lived for seventeen years after his two terms as President. During those years his fortune and the home he was still building declined and finally became ruins. Not only was his extensive hospitality a drain on his finances, but the money he loaned was never returned, and the notes he had signed for friends began to fall due.

Another reason for the disappearance of his money was the University of Virginia. He began building it in 1779, while he was governor of the state. With his usual thoroughness he planned the buildings, set up the courses of instruction, and even suggested rules of behavior for the students.

When at times Virginia refused to spend any more money on the university, Jefferson supplied the funds. The college was in the valley below Monticello, and Jefferson would sit at a window in his study for hours, a telescope to his eye, watching the work progress. When he noticed that his plans were not being followed, he would mount his horse and ride down the mountain to set things right.

The university has flourished and is one of the finest places of learning in the United States. It was one of Jefferson's proudest achievements. When a few years before his death he wrote the epitaph for his tombstone, he made no mention of having been president. Instead, he ordered that the carving should read: HERE WAS BURIED THOMAS JEFFERSON, AUTHOR OF THE DECLARATION OF INDEPENDENCE, OF THE STATUTE OF VIRGINIA FOR RELIGIOUS FREEDOM, AND THE FATHER OF THE UNIVERSITY OF VIRGINIA.

At last early in 1826 total ruin faced the man who had been the guiding light of the Revolution and the builder of a new nation. The final blow came when he was told that he, who had fed so many thousands, had not enough money to pay a small grocery bill.

Jefferson was eighty-three years old. His health had faded, and he realized he didn't have long to live. The notes he had signed for friends who did not repay amounted to more than $100,000, a tremendous sum in those days. He tried, to the best of his failing strength and mind, to repay that money before he died.

The only friend or relative who stood beside him in those last days was Jefferson Randolph, one of his grandsons. Between them they planned to hold a national raffle, the prize to be his beloved Monticello. He was willing to give up the home of his dreams to satisfy his creditors. But the raffle failed. People had forgotten Thomas Jefferson. He was left alone in the home he had labored so hard to build.

During July 1826 he became so weak he could not leave his bed. He accepted death, but he wanted to postpone it until July 4, the fiftieth anniversary of the Declaration of Independence. On the night of July 3 he fell into a coma. At times he awoke and feebly asked, "Is it yet the fourth?"

Only Jefferson Randolph and Jupiter were by his

bedside during those last hours. Both the white and the black man kept their eyes on the slowly moving hands of the clock. They knew how much the frail man in the bed wanted to live until those hands passed the hour of midnight.

At last, at four o'clock in the morning of July 4, 1826, he awoke again and asked, "Is it yet the fourth?" When they answered, "Yes," Jefferson smiled and drew his last breath.

A few weeks later Monticello was put up at auction.

The magnificent mansion had many owners during the following years. None of them took care of it or realized what it represented. Some of the owners were farmers, who kept cattle in the once lovely rooms. Others simply left it abandoned until, as Jupiter said later, "There was hardly a shingle left on the roof."

Then in 1923 after the property had lain in ruins for nearly a hundred years, some interested citizens began to realize what an important part of our heritage was represented by that house on the hill, and they began a campaign to raise money to buy the property and restore it to its former beauty. It wasn't easy. But the members of the Thomas Jefferson Memorial Foundation were determined. By 1930 they obtained the necessary funds, and Monticello began the long climb back to life.

Now, at last, the house on the hill is restored. Thousands of people from all lands journey there to pay honor to the genius of the American who built it and to the man who not only wrote the Declaration of Independence but passed on to his countrymen the love of democracy.

The house is peaceful now. Guards and guides take care of it. But there is one place where few tourists go. The Honeymoon Cottage at the end of the right hand terrace is often neglected and overlooked by the public. To many it is just a small cottage at the end of an elaborate estate. But it is more than that. It is the heart and spirit of the mansion on the mountain, and some say it is never unoccupied.

Jupiter, who lived close to the property until he died, began the story. He claimed that at night he often saw leaping flames from the fireplace reflected in the tiny windows. And, he was sure, those flames appeared more brightly during snow storms.

There are those there now who say the same.

THE
PHANTOM RIDERS
OF THE
PONY EXPRESS

In northern Kansas near the town of Hanover, there stands a mysterious, old, wooden building. It is supposed to be filled with the spirits of a strange breed of men. But it also contains spirits that never were human. It is called the Hollenberg Station. That ancient wooden building was one of the relief-stops on the famous Pony Express trail that stretched for 2,000 miles over lonely prairies and tall mountains from Missouri to California.

The Pony Express era was one of the most romantic and exciting in our nation's history. The riders were a special breed of men, and the ponies they rode were special, too.

In his book, *Roughing It*, Mark Twain described meeting one of those swift riders on the old Oregon-California trail in 1860.

Away across the dead level of the prairie a black speck appears against the sky, and it is plain that it moves ... In a second or two it becomes a horse and rider, rising and falling, rising and falling—sweeping toward us nearer and nearer—growing more and more distinct, more and more sharply defined—nearer and still nearer, and the flutter of hoofs comes faintly to the ear—another instant and, with a 'Hallooo!' and a wave of the rider's hand, the man and the horse burst past our excited faces, and go winging away like a belated fragment of a storm! So sudden is it all, and so like a flash of unreal fancy, but for the flakes of white foam left quivering and perishing on a thrown mail sack , . . . we might have doubted whether we had seen any actual man and horse at all . . .

Swift, lean ponies and equally lean young riders made the trip from St. Joseph, Missouri, to Sacramento, California, a distance of approximately 2,000 miles, in an average of ten days. Some famous riders made the trip in only eight days, averaging 250 miles every twenty-four hours.

From 100 to 120 young, wiry, experienced riders were employed, and eighty of them were in the saddle at all times. One at a time, several hours apart, forty riders started east from Sacramento, while forty more riders sped their mounts west from St. Joseph.

Their route was carefully planned. Going west it followed the Oregon-California trail across northern Kansas, then to the Platte River in Nebraska. From there the riders sped on to Fort Kearny, Fort Laramie, Fort Bridger, and on to Salt Lake City. The trail crossed Nevada and the high Sierra Mountains, and down to Sacramento, and the shores of the Pacific Ocean.

Every fifteen miles there was a relay station. There a rider would leave his foam-flecked, panting horse and mount a fresh one. A half mile or so from the next station the rider would give a high whoop or a coyote-call so that by the time he pulled to a stop in a cloud of dust, his fresh pony would be waiting for him.

At every third station a new rider would take over. The exhausted one would have some food and coffee, then rest for an hour or two, before leaping into the saddle again, relieving another rider.

Each man rode at least one hundred miles every day. They rode by day and night, in sunshine and storms. No matter if it hailed or snowed or if hostile Indians blocked the trail, they pressed on, riding as fast as their ponies could carry them, because in their saddlebags were letters and telegrams that were important to the growth of the new country. Then as now, "through sleet and snow and darkest night" the mail had to go through.

Before the beginning of the Pony Express the railroad and telegraph stopped at St. Joseph. From there commerce and communication to the Far West depended on the "Conestogas," the canvas-covered wagons used by the pioneers, or stagecoaches. But even stagecoaches had to stop to pick up or deliver people and freight, and the trip to California took an average of twenty-two days.

That was too slow. A growing, bustling new country required that news and documents should travel faster. The railroad was being pushed west mile after weary mile, and telegraph poles were being erected across the prairies and mountains. But it would be several years before either method of communication would be completed. A quicker way was needed and at once.

And so the Pony Express was born. It was decided

that a small man, riding a fast pony at breakneck speed, with frequent changes of mounts and riders, could cut the time in half. The Pony Express did exactly that.

The riders were selected carefully. They had to be young and small but of great physical strength. They were paid fifty dollars a month, plus room and board. Three hundred and twenty station keepers and helpers were hired, and they were also paid fifty dollars a month, plus room and board.

Each rider and station keeper had to sign a pledge: "I agree not to use profane language, not to get drunk, not to gamble, not to treat animals cruelly, and not to do anything a gentleman would not do."

The riders dressed simply, usually a buckskin shirt and cloth trousers tucked into high boots. They carried two revolvers, a supply of cartridges, and a knife. Rifles were not permitted, because they added weight and would cut down the speed.

The ponies wore the lightest of saddles. Mail was carried in a leather saddlebag, called a *mochila*, which contained four *cantinas* (boxes of hard leather), one in each corner so that one was behind and one in front of each leg of the rider.

The saddle and saddlebag weighed between twelve and fourteen pounds. Only twenty pounds of mail was carried. Letters and documents were written on the thinnest paper. The charge was $5.00 for each half-ounce letter, and $6.90 for a ten-word telegram. These rates were in addition to the regular United States postage.

Of course the ponies were exceptional. They were selected for stamina and speed. All were bred in the desert and were as thin and strong as their riders.

Great care was taken of these animals. After running at full gallop for fifteen miles they were, of course, exhausted. When a pony was replaced by a fresh mount at a station, it was slowly walked, as race horses are today so it could relax and regain its breath. Then it was rubbed down, fed, and allowed to rest until it was time for it to take to the trail again.

Of course, as with all carefully planned schedules, unexpected accidents and interruptions occurred. One rider named Jim Moore had a route that stretched for 140 miles across prairies and mountains. At the end of that run going east, he would rest for a day, then make the return journey of 140 miles to the station from where he had started.

On one occasion when Moore arrived at the end of his 140-mile run, he was told that the rider who was to make the return trip had been hurt in a fight and was unable to ride. He drank some coffee, filled his pockets with "jerky," the dried meat of buffalo, mounted a fresh pony and began the return journey. He spared neither himself nor his mounts and rode the 280 miles in twenty-two hours. He was given a gold watch and a certificate for his performance.

"Pony Bob" was another famous Pony Express rider. It was he who carried the news of the election of Abraham Lincoln. He rode 120 miles in less than eight hours and changed horses twelve times. During one stretch of his ride he was ambushed by Indians, and an arrow struck him in the jaw. He lost six teeth, but he brought the message through.

Perhaps the most famous of all Pony Express riders was William F. Cody, who later became known as "Buffalo Bill." When he rode for the Pony Express he was a lad of fourteen. However, even at that age he was strong and experienced in all the dangers of the West.

At first he was given only short routes, no more than fifteen miles a day. Then he began riding forty-five miles every day. Finally he galloped over some of the longest routes between St. Joseph and Sacramento.

Young Bill Cody also held the record for the longest ride in Pony Express history, when he carried the inaugural address of President Abraham Lincoln 320 miles in twenty-one hours and forty minutes.

Cody had another experience that is in the records of the Pony Express. Although only letters and telegrams were usually carried by the riders, there were rare occasions when even more valuable items were in the saddlebags.

At one time a very large sum of money had to be taken to California. By the time the money was in Cody's saddlebag there were rumors that bandits knew about it and would lie in wait for the rider. Cody's solution was simple. He realized that one lone rider would be no match for a group of desperate men, who would kill at the slightest provocation. Therefore he placed the money *under* the saddle, hidden in the blanket that lay between the leather and the skin of the horse. The real saddlebag, holding only paper, was in plain sight.

When he changed mounts at relay stations he made sure that the blanket containing the money was always under the new saddle. During the last lap of his journey bandits did stop him. He calmly handed over the saddlebag and continued on his way. He arrived in Sacramento on time with the money, leaving behind a group of robbers puzzling over a bag of blank paper.

While Bill Cody and other Pony Express riders dared the dangers of the long trails to the Far West, the telegraph and railroads were pushing on mile after mile across the prairies and mountains. By October 1861 the thin wires of the telegraph reached Sacramento and San Francisco, and the need for the spirited ponies and courageous riders of the Pony Express disappeared. But those few years demonstrated the bravery and resourcefulness of the American spirit in time of need, just as American courage and imagination have found solutions to other problems that have seemed to slow the growth of our great country from time to time.

A Kansas newspaper printed these words when the Pony Express disappeared: "It was thought that . . . the pony had accomplished wonders when he gave us communication with the Pacific coast in six to seven days. But now the pony has become a thing of the past—his last race is run. Without sound of trumpets, celebrations, or other noisy demonstrations, the slender telegraph wire has been stretched from ocean to ocean."

One of the most important Pony Express stations in Kansas was 123 miles west of St. Joseph. It was called the Hollenberg Station because it was located on a ranch owned by a man named Garet H. Hollenberg.

It was a long, frame, two-story building. On the first floor was the store, post office, tavern, and living quarters for the station-keeper's family. The second floor was a huge sleeping room for the Pony Express riders and the drivers of the overland stages. Near the main building was a shelter for more than 100 horses, fresh mounts for the Pony Express riders and various stagecoaches that stopped there.

Wagon trains, making their slow way to Oregon and California, stopped at the Hollenberg Station for food, feed for their animals, clothing, and all the other supplies needed for the long journey to the Far West. The people in those wagon trains knew this would be the last main stop until, after weary months of travel, they would at last see the placid waters of the Pacific Ocean.

For several years after the Pony Express was discontinued, the Hollenberg Station serviced wagon trains and stagecoaches, but eventually the railroad and time made it a thing of the past. Eight years after the last Pony Express rider galloped into the Hollenberg Station, the town of Hanover was formed, near the wooden structure that had seen so much of our early history.

Some of the people of Hanover never forgot that they were the guardians of an important part of our heritage. In the city park there is a statue commemorating the Pony Express riders. And in 1941 the Kansas legislature provided funds to buy the old Hollenberg Station and seven acres of land surrounding it. The building has been restored and is operated as a museum.

Every day visitors tour the old building and look with wonder and pride at relics of a time when brave men and women pushed slowly westward to make new homes in a new country.

But a building that has been a part of so much exciting history can never really die. There are stories told by those who wander through the park at night of hearing the neighing of horses and the staccato beat of po-nies' hoofs as they gallop down long-forgotten trails.

Some say that the mournful cry of a coyote can some-times be heard—always in the distance—as if a phantom rider is letting the station know that he will soon be there in a swirling cloud of dust, ready to swing astride a fresh pony and begin the dashing gallop to the next station.

The old Oregon-California trail is now a busy high-way. But there are some who say that at night on quiet stretches, they sometimes hear the sound of pounding hoofs and a faint "Hallooo!" as something passes them with the speed of wind.

It *could* be a gust of wind. But it also could be a phantom Pony Express rider, spurring his straining horse, east or west, to the next "station."

THE
CREEPING HOUSE

Most haunted houses have only one ghost, sometimes two, rarely more, but there is one house that has thousands of ghosts as guests. It is the mysterious Winchester mansion in San José, California.

The Winchester was the most famous rifle used in conquering the West. Many thousands of men, women and children, mostly Indians, died because of that firearm. It was also the most deadly weapon used during the Civil War when thousands of soldiers were slain by its bullets. Each gun, it is claimed, cost the lives of dozens of people.

By making and selling that rifle the Winchester Arms Company earned millions of dollars. Some historians might call the Winchester fortune, "blood money." No wonder those who used it or were touched by it are said to have had feelings of guilt. And no wonder hordes of ghosts followed it wherever it went.

Those throngs of ghosts came to rest (if ghosts can ever rest) in a 160-room mansion in a small California town.

In 1862 Sarah Pardee married William Wirt

Winchester, the son of the man who manufactured the famous Winchester Repeating Rifle. Their only child Annie Pardee died a month after birth from a mysterious illness. Mrs. Winchester was heartbroken. She was sure the souls of those who had been killed by the Winchester Rifle had placed a curse on those who bore that name. She was even more convinced of that curse when her husband died.

She always had been interested in the occult, the mysteries of the spirit world. One spiritualist she visited told her that the only way she could save her own life was to move to the West and build a house. As long as she continued to build, she would live.

Mrs. Winchester sincerely believed what the spiritualist told her. In 1884 to appease the avenging spirits of the dead she so desperately feared, she moved to the small town of San José, California. There she bought an old eight-room house on six acres of land.

She had a fortune of twenty million dollars and was willing to spend every cent of it if necessary to keep the angry ghosts from killing her. She immediately began to build on to the old house. She hired eighteen carpenters and twelve gardeners, who worked around the clock for thirty-eight years, hammering and sawing, planting and pruning, all day and all night, seven days a week. The result is a sprawling mansion of approximately 160 strange rooms. There are 10,000 windows, forty bedrooms, thirteen bathrooms, forty staircases, and nine kitchens.

Mrs. Winchester was obsessed with the number 13. The stairways have thirteen treads, and on one of them the steps are only two inches high! Almost all the rooms are made up of thirteen panels. The chandeliers in them have thirteen lights. When she ordered more hanging lamps for the additional rooms she was building and they had only twelve lights, she would have one of her electricians add one more light to make thirteen. All the rooms have thirteen windows, and if it was necessary to make that number, more windows were added, *even into inside walls!* When possible, each window had thirteen panes. Most of the thirteen bathrooms have glass doors, so there was no privacy. There is one room that has only trapdoors. Another room has a skylight built into the floor. There are secret passages, many that lead only to blank walls. Many of the forty stairways lead nowhere; some end against solid ceilings. Some of the doors on the second floor open only into thin air. There are five different heating systems and three elevators.

Each day Mrs. Winchester and her foreman would stroll around the property. Often she would order some of the things that had been built during the night to be torn down, changed, or something else built over them. During those strolls she would stop and draw new plans, sometimes sketching them on the backs of old envelopes or paper bags. And so the work went on, day after day, night after night.

The grounds of the house were just as strange. The first job given to the twelve gardeners was to plant a six-foot-high cypress hedge around the entire six acres. Mrs. Winchester wanted no one *alive*, who was not in her employ, to see what she was doing.

The gardeners labored as hard on the six acres as the

carpenters did inside the house. They made straight paths, paths that intertwined, and paths that led nowhere. Small orchards, bearing all kinds of fruit, were planted. Trees of every exotic type stood guard over ornate fountains that spewed water into the sky twenty-four hours a day.

One of the highlights of the gardens was a statue of an Indian, Chief Little Fawn, who was depicted firing arrows at hidden enemies. This statue was erected by Mrs. Winchester as atonement for and a reminder of the many thousands of peaceful Indians who had been killed by the bullets fired from the Winchester Repeating Rifles.

Here, too, Mrs. Winchester made daily visits. She strolled along the winding paths with her head gardener, making changes and ordering new work done. The six acres became a fairyland of greenery and flowers.

Many rooms in the growing mansion were filled with exotic and expensive materials, waiting to be used as other, more elaborate rooms were added. Selected rooms contained only stained glass doors and windows, some of them with jewels set in their colorful frames. The windows of other rooms were filled with concave and convex glass. Mrs. Winchester even designed a special type of glass in which was imbedded her favorite spider-web pattern. These panes were used in many openings in the outside walls of the house.

Other rooms contained rolls of embossed French wallpaper, some of it a quarter of an inch thick and very expensive, even in those days. There were rooms stacked with paintings; others were filled with ornate ornaments of copper, gold, and silver—all waiting to be placed in rooms that were being added to the mansion, day after day.

Vast as the construction was, Mrs. Winchester knew where every nail and screw was kept. On one occasion she told her foremen to repair one of the gates on the property. It required six nails. When she inspected the finished work she asked him where he had obtained the "yellow" nails.

"They're copper ones I found in a drawer in one of the toolrooms," he told her.

She shook her head. "Those are solid gold," she said. "I'm saving them for a special purpose. Please replace them with other nails."

During those thirty-eight years of constant building, Mrs. Winchester purchased the materials for her growing mansion from suppliers in the East and even in European countries. Railroad cars filled with stone, wood, and other construction materials would lie on the tracks at San José until they could be moved to the property.

For smaller items and personal things, she shopped by automobile. She never stepped out of the car, never entered a store. However the shopkeepers were delighted to bring their merchandise out to the curb where she would either order or reject it. She had two huge Pierce-Arrow cars, each painted lavender and gold.

She was a lonely woman, having only her memories and plans as companions. However, some of that loneliness might have been the result of something that was said to have happened a few years after she came to San José and began to build her strange mansion.

The story goes that she decided to give a reception for her new neighbors. The invitations were engraved in gold, and hundreds were sent to people in the area. There was to be a fabulous dinner with delicacies ordered from almost every section of the country. Even a famous orchestra was imported for the event. Mrs. Winchester waited until midnight. *But no one came.*

Old-timers in San José say that story isn't true. But the fact is that from then on Mrs. Winchester entertained no guests, not live ones, anyway.

Even in 1903 when President Theodore Roosevelt passed through San José and called at the Winchester Mystery Mansion, he was turned away with the message that "the house was not open to strangers."

Then who were the guests she entertained?

According to stories told by some of the townspeople and by workmen who labored on the strange building, the guests were the spirits of the dead Indians and soldiers she feared so much. One of the strangest rooms in the mansion was "The Blue Room," or "The Seance Room." No one but Mrs. Winchester was permitted to enter it. And it was in that room, so it is believed, that the spirits gathered nightly. They were summoned at midnight by the tolling of a bell in one of the towers on top of the mansion. At two o'clock in the morning the bell tolled again, and the spirits departed until the bell called to them again the next night.

During those two hours the strains of organ music could be heard by passersby in the street. There *are* several organs in the house, and Mrs. Winchester was a very good musician. But she had arthritis in her fingers, and the affliction was so severe she could hardly hold a pencil with which to make the plans she was constantly creating or changing. If that were so, then who played the organs night after night? Did she do it to exercise her stiff fingers, or were the keys manipulated by ghostly hands?

When Mrs. Winchester died in 1922 at the age of 85, there was enough building material left on the property to continue construction for another thirty-eight years. The furnishings and ornaments in the house were removed to a warehouse and auctioned off. Six moving vans were used eight hours a day for six weeks to transport the material. The empty house was purchased a year later by local people, and an admission fee was charged to visit the strange dwelling. Then on May 13 (again that magic number), 1974 the Winchester Mystery House officially became a California Historical Landmark, and restoration was started.

Strange as the Winchester Mystery House was at the end of its first thirty-eight years, *there is something still more strange about it now.*

There never were any blueprints of the house, so no one knows exactly what was built, when, or how. But some people who knew the place then and have visited it now believe that the sprawling structure is larger than they remember it to have been. Unfamiliar rooms and staircases appear to have been added, *as if the structure has grown by itself.*

Could it be that the spirit of the woman who began it and the spirits of the thousands she tried to appease have given the house a life of its own? Does it quietly, at night, continue to creep over those six acres?

THE
PHANTOM ZOO
OF SAGAMORE HILL

Most haunted houses have ghosts that were human when they were alive, but some houses are inhabited by other kinds of phantoms. A building called Sagamore Hill on Oyster Bay, Long Island, is said to shelter a strange variety of apparitions.

Sagamore Hill was the home of Theodore Roosevelt, the twenty-sixth president of the United States. He was only forty-two years of age when he was inaugurated.

He built Sagamore Hill when he was twenty-five years old and lived in it for thirty-five years until he died there at the age of sixty. Although he traveled to almost all parts of the world and held office in many cities, he never stayed long away from the home he loved. And it was in that home that more decisions were made, affecting the well-being of the United States, than in any other family residence. That was what Sagamore Hill was—the residence of a family, a most loving family.

No unhappy ghosts haunt the house that still stands overlooking the beauties of Oyster Bay. But other things that once were alive, but now are long dead, are said to roam through the rooms at night. To understand that house it is necessary to try to understand the man who built it, lived in it, and died in it. He was a man of paradoxes. Although he came from a wealthy family, he spent most of his life fighting what he called "the criminally rich people." And although he hated war and was aware of the terrible things that happened to countries and their people when they engaged in armed conflict, he is known for a famous sentence, "Speak softly, but carry a big stick." He sincerely believed that, horrible as war was, there were times when it was necessary in order to defend the principles of freedom.

He was a family man with six children, a wife, and a home he loved, yet he was almost constantly traveling to far parts of the world.

Finally, the greatest paradox of all was that although he was one of the most famous hunters of "big game," he was also the first and most important conservationist of our country. It was during his administration as president that he organized a National Conservation Commission and increased our national forest from 43 to 194 million acres. Because of his efforts we have many of the national parks we enjoy today.

There is a logical reason why he hunted elephants and lions in Africa, and buffalo, bear, and elk in the North and Far West. In those days, more than seventy-five years ago, no one realized that in time the wild animal population of the earth would be in danger of extinction. Exactly the opposite was believed. It was thought there were too many animals and that they were increasing so fast they were becoming a danger to themselves. The herds of wild animals in Africa, South America, and our Far West, were becoming so large that there was not enough food for all of them. To kill some, so that others might survive, was the reason why men like Roosevelt and others, who could afford the expense of travel, thought there was nothing wrong in killing a few of those animals. Being the type of man he was, Theodore Roosevelt would have taken the lead in protecting the world's wildlife, if he had known the danger of extinction they would face within the next century.

If one word could be used to describe Theodore Roosevelt's entire life, that word would be—vigor. He was weak and sickly as a child, but through strenuous exercise and will power, he became a healthy, robust man. He enjoyed the "rough life," sleeping at night under the stars, wrapped in a blanket, or hiking miles through unknown country.

Yet he was a scholar, too. He loved books, and one was in his pocket wherever he went. He wrote constantly by the light of a campfire or in his study at Sagamore Hill. During his lifetime the titles of books, essays, and stories he wrote totaled more than 3000.

In 1880 Theodore Roosevelt, just elected to the State Assembly of New York, bought 155 acres of wooded land on the shores of Oyster Bay, which had been part of the tribal lands of Sagamore Mahannis, Chief of the Matinecosk Indians. Roosevelt then married Alice Lee, whom he had met and courted while he was a student at Harvard. Together they planned the home they would live in for the rest of their lives.

But three years later he experienced the first and greatest tragedy of his life. His wife died, two days after giving birth to their first child Alice and before the home on Sagamore Hill was completed. Roosevelt was heartbroken. To try to get away from his grief he left politics and bought, unseen, a ranch in the Far West in a section called the Dakota Badlands. His sister Anna supervised the final construction of Sagamore Hill and took care of his daughter.

For three years Roosevelt lived, to the full, the rough life of a cowboy. He herded cattle, hunted in the mountains and prairies for his food, and even fought hostile Indians. But his energy would not let him stay in one place very long. He came back to the East and married a childhood playmate, Edith Carow. They moved into Sagamore Hill, and Roosevelt began to furnish the place with the heads and skins of animals he had hunted in the West, South America, and Africa. But again he became restless, and in 1895 when he was offered a job with the New York City Police Department that other men, more cautious, had refused, he jumped at the chance to clean up the very corrupt organization. In two years he made that department a model of efficiency and honesty.

Then in 1897 William McKinley, twenty-fifth president of the United States, asked Roosevelt to be his assistant secretary of the Navy. That was the job that opened the way to Roosevelt's greatest adventure and made the name "Teddy" Roosevelt world famous.

For several years before 1898 Cuba, a possession of Spain, had sought freedom, but Spain refused to give up its hold on the island or even to listen to the petitions of the Cubans for more humane treatment. The Spanish government began to imprison and sometimes kill thousands of Cubans who asked for their freedom. Finally Cuba appealed to the United States to negotiate with Spain, but the Spanish government refused even to talk about the situation.

In January 1898 President McKinley sent the small battleship, *Maine*, to Havana to assure the safety of the Americans who were living there. Less than three weeks later Spanish divers attached bombs to the hull of the ship and blew it up, killing 260 American sailors. "Remember the *Maine!*" became a rallying cry for Americans, and on April 21, 1898 President McKinley reluctantly asked Congress to declare that a state of war existed between the United States and Spain.

Theodore Roosevelt immediately resigned as assistant secretary of the Navy, because President McKinley had ordered that three regiments of cavalry be assembled to go to Cuba, and Roosevelt wanted to organize one of them. He knew exactly what type of men he wanted in his regiment. He sent letters to all the cowboys, Indians, and frontiersmen he had met in the West, asking if they wanted to join him. The response was one hundred percent. His old friends, and hunting companions joined him on May 16 in San Antonio, Texas. It was a strange regiment. Although officially known as the First U.S. Volunteer Cavalry, they were soon being called "Teddy's Rough Riders."

There was no saluting, no marching, nor any of the other regular army procedures. They were simply 1200 men who had known danger, were not afraid of death, and were loyal to the stout little man who wore thick glasses and whom they called "the little Colonel." The "Rough Riders" performed exactly as Roosevelt had expected.

One of the objectives of the American forces was San Juan Hill, gateway to the city of Santiago, but there was a delay in making the attack, and Roosevelt became restless. Against the orders of his superiors, Lieutenant Colonel Roosevelt led his strange regiment in a charge up that hill and captured it.

Soon afterwards Spain asked for a truce, and the war ended. Part of the peace agreement guaranteed Cuba's freedom.

Roosevelt and his "Rough Riders" returned to the United States as heroes. Even a famous doll called "Teddy Bear," was named after the small fat man whose eyes were so weak he had gone to Cuba with twelve extra pairs of glasses, some of them sewn into his hat.

William McKinley was running for a second term as president, and he immediately selected Theodore Roosevelt as his running mate. McKinley was elected president in 1901, but on September 14 of that year an assassin shot and killed him, and Theodore Roosevelt became president of the United States. In 1904 he was elected to a second term.

Almost all the men who are elected to the presidency immediately move their families into the White House, and that is their home during their terms in office, but not Theodore Roosevelt. He lived in Washington most of the time, and his family was there, too, for special occasions. But every moment he could spare from duties that required his presence in the capital, he and his family returned to Sagamore Hill. The friendly, sprawling residence that overlooked Oyster Bay was often called "the second White House."

It was there in the study he loved that he held important meetings, not only with members of his cabinet, but with some of the leaders of the most powerful countries of the world. It was at Sagamore Hill he signed papers recognizing the Republic of Panama when it sought independence from Colombia. And it was at the desk in that study he pored over the plans that eventually became the Panama Canal.

It was in his library that Roosevelt met with Serge Witte, the Russian envoy, and Count Komura, the Japanese delegate, to lay the foundation for the peace that stopped the Russo-Japanese War. It was called "The Treaty of Portsmouth," but many journalists of that day referred to it as "The Treaty of Sagamore Hill."

Roosevelt was interested in everything new. While he was negotiating with the Russians and the Japanese news reached him that one of the Navy's experimental submarines, the *Plunger*, had slipped into Oyster Bay. Leaving the Russian and Japanese envoys having tea at Sagamore Hill, Roosevelt eluded the Secret Service men who were guarding him and went to the harbor. He spent two hours cruising beneath the waters of the bay, most of the time at the controls of the submarine. Later he said, "I can't remember so much fun crowded into two hours."

One time at Sagamore Hill, he was entertaining the emissary of the Empress Dowager of China. When the old mandarin left he complimented Roosevelt on the *fueng chuey* of the house.

"What's *fueng chuey*?" the president asked.

"It is the personality of a house that is hospitable to good spirits," the emissary replied, "and resistant to evil spirits. Your home has *fueng chuey.*"

Whatever it was, the house was a happy one. No matter what important visitors might be in the library or study, four o'clock was a special hour. If the president forgot, there would be a soft knock on the door, and one of his children would call, "It's four o'clock!"

The president would look at his watch and exclaim, "So it is!" Then he would ask to be excused. "We can talk later. I never keep the children waiting."

He would join his four sons, Teddy, Jr., Kermit, Archie, and Quentin, and two daughters, Alice and Ethel, for a hike, a swim, or a general romp on the lawn. He was a father first, all other matters took second place.

Then on a cold night, January 6, 1919, the vigor and energy that had sustained him for sixty years quietly faded away. He went to bed early that night after reading aloud to Mrs. Roosevelt as he usually did. It had been a happy evening. The First World War was over, and three of his sons would soon be returning from Europe. Quentin, the youngest, would not; he had been killed while flying over the German lines. Theodore Roosevelt had tried to take part in the great conflict, and 250,000 men across the nation had written letters saying they would follow him, but President Wilson denied permission to let him organize the regiments he had planned. He never awakened again. The spirit of "the little colonel" had fled.

Mrs. Roosevelt lived on at Sagamore Hill for another twenty-eight years. Two years after her death the home was purchased by the Theodore Roosevelt Association.

In 1963 Sagamore Hill was presented to New York City as a gift, and it is now open to the public.

Certainly happy ghosts must romp through the rooms and halls and over the spacious lawns of Sagamore Hill. Children and grandchildren must play games and follow their leader, a stout, hearty man who shouts "Bully!" and "Dee-lighted!" when things please him.

But what are the other phantoms that roam through the rooms and halls at night?

Just a glance into the twenty-two rooms of the sprawling home called Sagamore Hill will explain what they must be. Hanging from the walls and lying on the floors of every room are heads and skins representing almost all the animals that inhabit the earth, and some of the chairs have been made from tusks and horns, cleverly arranged to support the skins of lions and tigers. The entire house is a zoo of dead creatures. Many of the animals were killed by Roosevelt himself, long before there was concern that some of them would slowly disappear from the jungles and plains. Others were sent to him by kings and the heads of governments of many countries of the world.

But they *were* living things.

It's logical to suppose that at the end of the day, when the guards and guides have left Sagamore Hill to the quietness of the night, that the spirits of those animals do rise and prowl through the rooms of that home that has seen so much history.

No one has seen that phantom zoo at night, and only a few say they have heard them.

But those spirits are there. They *must* be there.

THE
WHITE-HAIRED SPIRIT
THAT CAN NEVER REST

Ghosts don't always haunt houses or buildings that are still standing. Phantoms don't need doors, windows, or even walls. Therefore they can and do haunt places where buildings or houses once stood, especially if those places witnessed scenes of terror and horror.

There is such a place in the small town of Harper's Ferry, West Virginia. Only markers are there now, but some who live near that place can verify that the ghosts of one of the most fascinating and extraordinary men in our history and his companions haunt that site now.

Even though that man was God-fearing and thought his acts were good, he created a scene of dread and fear that influenced the history of our nation. His name was John Brown.

What he did at Harper's Ferry helped cause the Civil War. It also made him the most popular man in the North, second only to President Abraham Lincoln. But what he did ended with him and his companions being hanged by their necks until they were dead.

John Brown was an abolitionist. He hated slavery.

He also was a religious man and sincerely believed it was against God's teachings that one man should own another man.

His father, too, hated slavery and was one of the operators of the "underground railway." This wasn't a railroad as we know them. It was a series of "stations" where runaway slaves were helped by night from place to place until they reached Canada, and freedom.

In those days before the Civil War, that was a dangerous thing to do. All the northern states had laws making the helping of escaped slaves illegal. Not only were the slaves returned to their owners in the South if caught, but the northerners who helped them were arrested, fined, and often sent to jail.

John Brown was born in Connecticut in 1800, but over the years he lived in many parts of the country. Sometimes he operated a "station" for his father; other times he was a salesman, farmer, or businessman. But always he searched for ways to help the Negroes in the South. He had twenty sons. Eight of them died in childhood; the others, when they grew to manhood, hated slavery as much as their father did.

After the death of his father, John Brown took his place as one of the operators of the "railway." As his sons grew older and married, he placed each one on a farm or in a small town along a route that led from the deep South to the Canadian border. In this way he managed to help hundreds of runaway slaves flee from station to station and on to freedom. However, when John Brown thought of the many thousands of Negroes in the South who were owned as if they were animals, he felt that saving them, one by one, was not enough. He wanted all of them to be free.

In 1855 he had an opportunity to do more for the cause of freeing slaves. In that year the vast territory of Kansas asked to be admitted to the Union as a state. But would it enter as a free state or as a slave state?

Its southern neighbor, Missouri, had been admitted to the Union as a slave state in 1821. The Missourians wanted the new state to be a slave state, too. It would mean they could sell their excess Negroes to Kansas, and also another slave state would give the South more representatives in Congress. That fact was very important. There had been debates in Washington about passing laws to control slavery. One law would prohibit the importation of Negroes from Africa. Another law would declare "free" all children born to blacks who now were slaves. It was important to the southern states that there should be enough "slave" votes in Congress to stop the passage of those laws.

There were many Kansans who hated slavery, and wanted their new state to be free. Also many people from neighboring northern states were anxious to prohibit slavery in Kansas. As the constitution for the new state was being debated in Topeka, the capital of the territory, those northern whites flocked into Kansas to do everything they could to make sure the new state would have laws against slavery. It soon became a vicious and cruel border war. Missourians would cross into Kansas and burn the farms of Kansans who were against slavery.

Then angry Kansans would attack the farms and homes of slave owners in Missouri.

That "Border War" was the opportunity John Brown had been looking for. In 1856 he and his sons moved to the village of Osawatomie in southern Kansas. From there they and some Kansans who considered John Brown their leader made frequent forays into Missouri, burning farms and killing livestock. On each raid they brought back slaves and started them on the underground railroad to Canada. But they didn't stop with only burning farms and rescuing slaves.

On the night of May 24, 1856 Brown and his group raided the farms of the Doyle and Wilkinson families and killed five people. Brown left a message at the smoking ruins: "This is a Free State warning to all pro-slavery people that the war will be a tooth for a tooth and an eye for an eye . ." The Missourians struck back at once. They attacked Osawatomie, killed one of Brown's sons, and burned the village to the ground.

Although Brown and his followers were religious and even read the Bible to one another every day, they were convinced that only by violence would all the slaves become free. And so the Border War went on, becoming more savage as the months passed.

During the next two years the Border War cost the lives of hundreds of men on both sides of the slavery question. The authorities of the Territory could do little to stop the killings and burnings. The land area was vast and sparsely settled. Also the debates in Topeka about how and when it would become a state had temporarily left the land almost lawless. The authorities in Missouri did nothing. They hoped the conflicts along the border would convince Kansans that they should enter the Union as a slave state.

Then on December 20, 1858 Brown and some followers made another daring raid deep in Missouri. They killed one plantation owner and escaped with eleven slaves. The Negroes were hidden near Osawatomie for several days while supplies were gathered then John Brown and his sons started with them on the long journey north to Canada. However, friends of the murdered slave owner pursued the fleeing group and finally caught up with them near the northern border of Kansas. Although Brown and his sons were outnumbered more than two to one, they fought so fiercely that the slave owners retreated. Eventually the eleven slaves found freedom in Canada.

By this time John Brown was convinced that Kansas would eventually enter the Union as a free state, and that "the work of the Lord" he had done in that territory was finished. (He was correct. On January 28, 1861 Kansas did enter the Union as a free state. It was only a month after December 24, 1860 when South Carolina became the first southern state to secede from the Union, and the Civil War began.)

Two years before Kansas joined the Union, John Brown decided it was time to put into action the great plan he had been dreaming about for many years. He would free *all* the Negroes in all the southern states.

John Brown was 59 years old when he put his daring

scheme into action. He was tall, lean, and burned brown by the sun. He appeared even taller because of a mop of white hair that stuck up on his head like the plumage of some strange bird. He also had a thick white beard that reached to his chest. But the most amazing and frightening things about him were his eyes. They were bright blue and burned in his brown face with a queer inner light. He looked like an angry prophet.

He made an impressive, even awe-inspiring appearance. And when in 1859 he went to Canada to raise funds and gather followers for his plan, he had no trouble finding groups of people who listened to his dream of freeing all the blacks that were held in captivity like animals.

What he wanted to do, he told them, was establish a base of operations somewhere in the mountains of West Virginia where escaped slaves could gather. There he and his men would train and prepare them for an invasion of the South. Once that operation was started, he told his listeners, he was certain all the slaves would rise up against their masters and join him.

He dreamed of a triumphant march into the South with jubilant Negroes joining his small army every mile. Eventually the entire South would be cleansed of the sin of slavery.

But first there would have to be an action, a daring action, an action that would accomplish two things; first, it would announce to all the slaves that their "Savior" was at hand; second, it would supply arms and ammunition to all who flocked to join him. That action would be to attack and capture the United States' Arsenal at Harper's Ferry on the borderline of the South.

The preparations of the assault were accomplished quietly. With the money he had been given by his Canadian supporters, Brown rented a farm in the mountains near Harper's Ferry. There he collected guns and ammunition and trained the twenty-eight men he had carefully selected to help him carry out the first part of his plan. Three of the men were his sons, five were Negroes, the rest were experienced fighters who had been with him in battles and raids in Kansas.

Near midnight on October 16, 1859 the twenty-eight men and their leader crept quietly to the outskirts of the little town of Harper's Ferry. Brown was easy to follow because as one of the survivors said, "His white hair and white beard were like beacons in the moonlight."

One by one the guards at the arsenal were overpowered and bound with ropes. Then the railway station was easily captured, because it was from there, by telegraph, that messages would be sent to all the South, telling of the successful attack, and announcing that all the slaves should revolt and join him.

But John Brown's plan was not yet completed. During the early hours of the morning his men knocked on the doors of many houses that surrounded the arsenal and captured sixty sleepy men and women. These were held as hostages in the armory to assure that no southerners would attack Brown's small force until the thousands of slaves he expected would flee to his side to be armed.

By early morning the telegraph messages had been sent North and South, and the entire country knew that the white-haired "prophet" had kept his word. The uprising of slaves had begun!

But that uprising was a complete failure. *Not one slave appeared!* For a day and a night John Brown waited. In his possession were enough rifles and ammunition to arm 10,000 Negroes, but no one came to use them. John Brown finally realized that his great plan had failed, and that he would have to pay the price for that failure.

He told his men that those who wished to should try to escape but that he would remain and die with his dream. Five of his companions slipped away into the darkness. The others, including his sons, stayed with him.

Brown also realized that the hostages he had taken were now useless. *They* couldn't make the slaves rally to his side. And his religious beliefs stopped him from killing innocent people. In groups of ten he released his captives to find safety in their homes. Then he and his companions waited.

On October 18 a detachment of marines, led by Colonel Robert E. Lee (who in less than two years would become General Robert E. Lee in charge of all the southern armies), attacked the arsenal and captured it. Nine of John Brown's men, including his sons, were taken prisoners, and four were killed. The old man himself was seriously wounded after the surrender by a soldier who accidentally discharged his rifle.

John Brown's wound was taken care of, but he was too weak to stand when his trial began nine days later. He was carried into the courtroom, and his bed was placed in front of the high podium of the judge. It was a short trial, and he was convicted of "treason and conspiring with slaves and other rebels, and for murder in the first degree." The sentence was death by hanging.

Telegrams and letters by the thousands poured from the North into the White House at Washington. Northern sympathizers considered the white-bearded old man a hero. He had struck the first blow against the sin of slavery. They demanded that he be freed or at least saved from death. More thousands of letters and telegrams came from the South. Southerners were alarmed that John Brown's plan for an uprising of the slaves *could* have been successful and that another man might try again to turn the slaves against their masters. But John Brown had been tried and convicted as a traitor and murderer, no matter how noble or religious his reasons. President James Buchanan ordered the execution to proceed.

Soon after dawn on a cold day, December 2, 1859, 1500 United States' marines formed a hollow square in an open field near the prison at Charlestown, Virginia. In the center of the square was a gallows.

A few minutes later a farm wagon, drawn by two white horses, entered the square. In the wagon was a plain pine coffin. Seated on the coffin, his white hair bared to the sun, was John Brown. Two soldiers stood beside him. The wagon creaked to a stop within a few yards of the gallows, and the man with the white hair and long white beard climbed down to the ground.

John Brown's wound was almost healed, and he could stand. For a few seconds he glanced around at the ranks of soldiers, then he looked at the sky. The rising sun made his hair and beard look like a halo of white.

"I'm glad it's a beautiful day," he said to one of his guards. Then, with a firm tread, he walked to the gallows and mounted the steps.

"Please do not make me wait too long," he said to the executioner who placed the rope around his neck.

At a signal from the commanding officer the drummers began the dreaded beat of the death march. At another signal an ax swung high into the air. For a second its bright blade glinted in the sunlight. Then it fell with a thud, cutting the rope. The body of John Brown fell through the trapdoor and swung slowly in the morning breeze. In a few days the rest of his companions, including his sons, were hanged on the same gallows.

The arsenal and armory were burned when Union forces occupied Harper's Ferry after the Civil War began in 1861. Now markers outline where they both once stood. But to the ghostly eyes of those who must haunt that place, those buildings are still there and must look as they did during those few terrible days in October 1859. And especially they must be real to the burning blue eyes of one old man with white hair like the plumage of a strange bird and a white beard hanging down to his chest.

Even during those horror-filled days, those who saw him then knew that he could never really die. They even composed a song about him, a song that was sung a-round thousands of campfires during the long years of the Civil War.

"John Brown's body lies a-mouldering in the grave.
"But his truth goes marching on."

That spirit is still marching and will continue to march until all people of all colors are free—everywhere.

THE
PHANTOM LINE
ON THE MISSION FLOOR

There is one building in the United States that is haunted by very special ghosts. They are the spirits of men whose heroic deeds in that place increased the size of our country by one-third in 1836.

The building is called the Alamo.

Alamo, in Spanish, means a cottonwood tree. When the low, mud-brick and stone building was built in 1718 it was surrounded by those lovely, tall trees. Its real name is Mission San Antonio de Valero. It still stands, not far from the downtown area of San Antonio, Texas.

On a cold morning, February 27, 1836, one hundred and eighty-three men, Texans all, crouched behind the stone walls of the building that had been a mission, but was now a fort. Although the men who had come there to fight called themselves "Texans," only a few of them had been born in that vast land. Most of them had traveled long miles from Kentucky, Virginia, and other states to help the Territory of Texas fight for its freedom from Mexico.

"Davy" Crockett, wearing his famous coon-skin cap,

was there. He had ridden night and day from Tennessee with other frontiersmen. Jim Bowie, inventor of the "Bowie" hunting knife, was there too with a band of hunters from Georgia. These men and others like them had one thing in common. They hated oppression and were willing to give their lives in Texas' struggle for independence.

What those men were waiting for at The Alamo was to meet and turn back a Mexican army under the leadership of General Santa Anna. That army, more than 4,000 strong, had crossed the river called the Río Grande. Its purpose was to capture and kill all Americans who were trying to make an independent territory of what was then known as a part of New Spain. The Americans had expected to be outnumbered, but not by so many.

On that winter morning the Mexican cannon began to bombard The Alamo. Late that night, scouts who had been spying on the Mexicans galloped their foam-covered horses through the wide gate of the fort.

"More Mexicans are crossing the river," they reported to Colonel William Travis, who was in command of the small force. "There are many thousands of them."

Colonel Travis was not yet thirty years old. He had been a lawyer in South Carolina but had come to Texas a few years before to take part in its revolution for independence. He was an excellent planner with a cool head in emergencies. He was also a fair man and believed in the truth. He called the Americans together in the chapel of The Alamo.

"Men," he told them, "we are outnumbered by many

more than I thought. We have very little supplies and ammunition. When Santa Anna attacks I'm sure all of us will die. I will stay here to the end, but you have a choice." With his sword he drew a line on the ground.

"Any of you who wish to leave may do so. This is your last chance. But those who want to stay here and die for the cause of liberty, step across this line to my side."

Only one man mounted his horse and rode out of the gate. All the rest stepped across the line. Jim Bowie, who was ill with fever, tried to get out of his cot but fell back, exhausted. "Don't leave me here, boys!" he called. "Help me across the line!" Several men put down their rifles and carried the sick man to the side of Travis

For twelve days the Mexican cannon hurled grape-shot into the square and solid balls of iron against the walls of The Alamo. And each day more Americans fell, wounded or dead. On the thirteenth day the Mexicans concentrated their cannon on one small section of The Alamo. By midday they had knocked a hole in one of the walls, and screaming Mexicans poured through it into the fort. The Americans who were still alive fought hand-to-hand with the yelling horde until only five could stand. These five men were brought to where Santa Anna sat on his black horse in the center of the square.

"Kill them," he ordered. "But don't waste bullets."

The five Americans were clubbed to death.

It was a massacre. That massacre of the 183 Americans at The Alamo was a direct result of another massacre, three hundred years before. In 1519 Hernando

Cortes and several hundred conquistadores landed on the coast of Mexico. In less than a year the Spaniards had murdered many thousands of the friendly Indians, called the Aztecs, and had added millions of square miles of Central and North America to the empire of the Spanish king, Charles I. For the next 300 years that immense territory was called "New Spain" and was governed by viceroys sent by the Spanish court.

Almost midway into that territory was the river, Río Grande. South of the river was Mexico, and north stretched a huge part of New Spain, called Tejas after a tribe of Indians by that name who lived there. As more Americans began to move into that lonely land, its name was gradually changed to Texas.

That land was lonely. Settlers from the east hauled their covered wagons across prairies and mountains to Oregon and California, where the land was lush. Few came to the hot, dry, endless plains of the Texas Territory, but some did come. And one man, Moses Austin, started the events that ended in the bloody massacre at The Alamo.

Moses Austin had come to Texas from West Virginia. He was fascinated with the wide prairies and dreamed of a time when the territory would become a new state in the Union. Austin didn't like being governed by a viceroy in Mexico City, who followed orders of a king thousands of miles away, but he realized that before Texas could become a state some important things would have to happen. First, more people would have to settle there. Then independence would come, and finally, statehood. He had a plan that might make that dream a reality, but it would have to wait until one more event occurred.

For ten years Mexico had tried to win freedom from Spain. At last in 1821 it succeeded. Mexico still controlled the Texas Territory, although there was danger that she might lose it. Now that Spain had given it up, one of the other European countries might try to claim it. France and England were rapidly and greedily expanding their empires. Surely the tremendous acreage of Texas would tempt them. But if more settlers came to Texas, built homes and had families, those new "Texans" would certainly fight if France or England made an attempt to rule them.

It was the perfect time for Moses Austin to go to Mexico City and present his plan to its first president, Augustin Iturbide. It was a simple plan. If Mexico wanted more people to come to Texas, then they should be given land on which to build their homes. Therefore, if he, Moses Austin, was given a large grant of land, he would advertise throughout the United States for settlers and would see that each family had enough land for a homestead. President Iturbide eagerly agreed, and Austin returned to Texas. But before he could put his plan into operation, he became ill and died.

However he left detailed notes explaining what he intended to do, and luckily his son, Stephen F. Austin, felt about Texas the same way he did. Stephen Austin began advertising for settlers, and soon families from various parts of the country drove their wagons into

Texas to take advantage of the Austin offer. The lovely city of Austin, capital of Texas, is named after Stephen and his father.

As Moses Austin had planned, his idea was good for Texas but bad for Mexico. More Americans did come into the territory, but, being Americans, they rebelled against any foreign country governing them. And that included Mexico.

For the next fifteen years the new Texans struggled for independence. And the Mexican government fought to keep the territory. Mexicans raided American settlements, and Americans attacked Mexican villages. Both sides of the Río Grande became bloody battlegrounds.

Then in 1830 Mexico passed a law prohibiting any more Americans from entering Texas. At the same time it gave large grants of land to wealthy Mexicans. That law turned the border fighting into an all-out war. Five years later angry Texans gathered at the town of San Felipe de Austin, the first village Stephen Austin had established. A Texas provisional government was organized, and Sam Houston was selected as "general of the armies of Texas."

Houston, a Virginian, had had a varied life before coming to the territory. He'd been an officer in the United States' Army, member of the United States' House of Representatives, and governor of Tennessee. His experience and advice were extremely valuable to the new government.

Santa Anna, who was now president of Mexico, sent an army to subdue the upstart Americans north of the Río Grande. This army, under the leadership of General

Cos, attacked San Antonio but was beaten back and forced to recross the river into Mexico. Santa Anna was furious. He organized a larger army and, with himself as general, once more crossed the Río Grande to "capture and kill" every American in the territory.

The "armies" of Texas were in three places. One was at San Antonio in the fort called The Alamo. Another, led by General Fannin, was at a town called Goliad. The third, under the command of Sam Houston, was near the San Jacinto River. Each force numbered only a few hundred men.

Santa Anna attacked The Alamo first, and after thirteen days' siege, massacred the 183 men in the fort. He then struck at Goliad, and captured General Fannin and 371 men. He held these Texans captives for twenty days, then ordered every one of them to be shot. Santa Anna was confident that the revolution was over. But there was one more man he had to capture and kill—Sam Houston. He turned his army toward the San Jacinto River.

The people of Texas were horrified by what had happened at The Alamo, even more than the murder of the men at Goliad. But they also were inspired. Across the prairies, like wildfire, swept the rallying cry, "Remember The Alamo!" Men flocked to join Sam Houston, and soon his forces numbered more than a thousand Texans.

Sam Houston had a plan he thought might work. Usually armies fought from morning until night, then rested until dawn, and began again. There were night raids, of course, but almost always enemies faced one another in daylight. Houston decided to fight another way, but he kept his plan secret, even from his men.

The Texas army waited at the San Jacinto River. Late in the afternoon of April 20 the advance units of Santa Anna's army appeared. The Texans had only two cannon. When the Mexicans came within range the cannons fired, killing several horses and a number of soldiers. The Mexicans fell back to their main force.

Everyone, Texans and Mexicans, were sure that the real fighting would begin early the next morning. But late that night two Texan scouts rode into camp with the news that Santa Anna was getting reinforcements. Houston was sitting under a tree, munching his favorite food, kernels of corn.

"How far away are these reinforcements?" he asked. "And how soon do you think they'll get here?"

"They're not mounted. They should be here day after tomorrow," was the answer.

"Then Santa Anna will be alone tomorrow, and he won't want to fight." General Houston rolled into his blanket and was asleep at once.

The next morning there was no activity in the Mexican camp. They were waiting for the reinforcements. Santa Anna wanted to make sure he could end the revolution in one battle. At four o'clock in the afternoon Sam Houston mounted his white horse and called the Texans together.

"Boys," he shouted so that every man could hear, "Over there they're having what they call a "siesta." They'll feel real groggy when they wake up, and then they'll start to make their supper. So maybe this might be the right time to pay them a visit."

And that's how the revolution was won. When the Americans crept up to the camp of the Mexicans late that afternoon, they saw guns stacked, soldiers sleeping, and meat slowly turning on spits over campfires. It was over in eighteen minutes. Those soldiers who didn't run, were killed. Some Mexicans ran straight into the slowly marching reinforcements, told them of the "thousands" of wild Texans who had attacked, and joined that force as it hurried back across the Río Grande.

Santa Anna, in blue bathrobe and red slippers, rushed from his tent, saw there was no hope of rallying his army, and fled on his black horse. The casualty list showed 630 Mexicans killed, 208 wounded, and several more hundreds taken prisoner. Only nine Americans lost their lives, and thirty were wounded.

The next morning Sam Houston was sitting under a tree. His foot had been shattered by a bullet during the fighting, and a doctor was changing the bandages. Suddenly two tall Texans appeared, yanking between them a frightened little man in a blue bathrobe and red slippers.

"We thought he was just another Mexican and were putting him in the stockade, but he says he's Santa Anna."

Sam Houston held out his hand. Kernels of corn covered the palm.

"Did you think you could win against men who love freedom so much they'll travel and fight on rations like these?"

When Santa Anna begged for mercy, the Texas general told him, "You should have thought of that at The Alamo and Goliad."

But Americans are merciful. Santa Anna and the other Mexican prisoners were returned to Mexico the next year, when the Republic of Texas was recognized by the United States, France, and England.

But Mexico still refused to agree to Texas' independence. Raiding parties continued to cross the Río Grande to burn and kill. Even in 1845 when Texas was admitted to the Union as the twenty-eighth state, Mexico refused to give up its claim to the territory. Finally, to save American lives, the United States sent a small military force to patrol the north bank of the Río Grande. Mexico immediately declared war. It was a short war. In six months American forces were in Mexico City.

The peace treaty gave the United States the entire Texas Territory. It included Texas, New Mexico, Arizona, Nevada, California, Utah, parts of what is now one third of our country.

But it was the desperate battle at the little mission and fort in San Antonio that resulted in the rallying cry—"Remember The Alamo!" and drew all of Texas together with the determination to win independence or die. It was during those thirteen days of siege that those 183 men gave their lives to light a tiny flame for freedom. That small flame has become a torch that blazes brighter as each year passes and has shed its light into dark places, wherever people are oppressed.

At San Jacinto there is a tall monument in memory of the Texans who were willing to die in the battle that turned back the Mexican army and led to independence and finally statehood.

The Alamo still stands. Of course it is filled with the

ghosts of the men who fought their last fight there and who died not knowing that giving their lives would accomplish the hope that was in each heart—freedom for the land they loved. But those ghosts know now, because their spirits can be felt everywhere within the stout walls that guard that sacred place.

There is one spot, though, that is more precious than all the others within that ancient fort. It is the chapel where Colonel Travis used his sword to draw a thin line on the floor. That thin line returns again and again. No matter how scuffed it becomes with the feet of the thousands of tourists who visit that hallowed place, it returns as fresh as if it has been newly drawn by a phantom sword.

THE
GOLDEN GHOSTS
OF EL DORADO

One bright morning in January 1848 a man named James Marshall was walking along a stream in northern California. Suddenly he stopped and stared. What had caught his eye was something gleaming in the water. He stooped and picked up what appeared to be a yellow stone. But it wasn't a stone.

It was a nugget of pure gold.

What James Marshall held in his hand eventually made some men rich and wrecked the lives of others. One of the results of finding that yellow stone is that one entire county in California is haunted, not only by the ghosts of men but by the spirits of complete towns. That county is called El Dorado, which means "The Gilded" in Spanish.

James Marshall was where he was when he picked up that piece of pure gold because of a man named John Sutter. Sutter had been born in Switzerland, but the lure of adventure brought him to California in 1840 when Mexico still controlled that territory. There was a law that prohibited foreigners from settling there, but Sutter had charm and determination, and soon he convinced the Mexican governor to give him a large grant of land. In return Sutter promised to cultivate the area and grow crops that would benefit the territory and Mexico

He lost no time in putting his scheme to work. He selected a spot near where the Sacramento and American Rivers met, hired some Indians, and began to build his empire. He called the place New Helvetia (New Switzerland); that place is now the city of Sacramento, capital of California.

First Sutter built a sturdy fort. Then he surrounded it with shelters for his workers. He built granaries, warehouses, stores and workshops. The settlement prospered, and at the end of seven years more than 1,000 people lived around "Sutter's Fort" and were dependent on Sutter for work and food. On his broad acres roamed 12,000 cattle, 2,500 horses, 1,500 pigs, and 10,000 sheep. Wheat, barley, rye, and other foods grew on more of his vast fields.

Sutter was king of his little empire. Servants fulfilled his wishes, and workers toiled so that he became ever more powerful and wealthy. But his greed for more power and riches caused the downfall of his domain, and resulted in his death as a lonely, forgotten, and poor man.

He decided to produce lumber so he could build more houses to expand his empire and to sell to the many new settlers who were coming into California. There were many forests in the area, but what was needed was a sawmill to convert those trees into finished wood for building. He was sure he could increase his fortune if he added lumber-making to his other enterprises.

One of Sutter's foremen was James Marshall, who had come to California from New Jersey to find opportunity in the new land. Marshall was a strange man and was avoided by the other workers because he believed he could see and talk with "spirits from another world." But he was a good worker, and Sutter trusted him. Marshall was given orders to select a spot somewhere along the American River and construct a sawmill.

He soon found the perfect place. Large stands of trees were nearby, and the river was narrow there, making the water flow swiftly. He immediately put a crew of Indians and white men to work building the mill. When it was almost finished they changed one of the channels of the river so it would flow through the building to produce the power that would move the huge mill wheels. It was while Marshall was inspecting that millrace that he found the nugget of gold.

He was quite sure it was gold, but he wanted to make certain. He didn't mention his discovery to the workmen, but gave orders that they should continue building the mill. Then he mounted his horse and rode to Sutter's office in New Helvetia.

Sutter wasn't very impressed with the nugget. He had plenty of wealth, and gold didn't interest him. But he, too, wanted to be sure it really was gold. He and Marshall put the nugget through some tests. They pounded it into a thin sheet, then melted it into a ball again. There were other experiments. The last one was to soak it in nitric acid. The nugget emerged unchanged from all the tests. Then Sutter, who had a good library, studied everything in it that concerned gold.

"It really *is* gold," he told Marshall at last.

But instead of being happy, Sutter was apprehensive. He knew that if the discovery of gold on his land became known, the workers would drop anything they were doing and rush to find more of it. He made Marshall swear to keep the discovery secret, then sent him back to finish the sawmill, but keeping a secret like that was impossible. It wasn't long before the news of finding gold at Sutter's Mill was passed from man to man.

The result was the great gold rush of 1849. Those who took part in it were called the "Forty-Niners." California and the United States were never the same again. The news of the discovery of gold in California swept across the country. Men in Boston, New York, and all other cities stopped what they were doing and started for California to make their fortunes. Doctors, lawyers, teachers, shopkeepers and adventurers left their homes and families to search for the yellow metal that would make their dreams come true.

To most of them California was the name of a land far, far away, almost on the other side of the world, and there were only three ways to get to it. You could buy a wagon and horses, load up with supplies, and begin the long, weary, and dangerous journey across the continent. You could buy passage on a sailing ship (if there was room), and make the perilous voyage around the southern tip of South America. Or you could find your way, by ship or wagon, to Panama, haul your supplies across the unhealthy isthmus to the Pacific Ocean, then try to find a way up the western coast of Mexico and southern California to the gold fields. All three ways were hazardous, especially for people who were used to cities and easy living.

But the lure of gold led them on. They started out by the thousands, and hundreds died on the way.

Many of them were killed crossing the Sierra Mountains, the last barrier to the West coast. Others died of strange fevers in Panama. Still more drowned at sea, fighting the high winds and waves when their ships tried to go around Cape Horn. But they were determined to get to the place where, they had heard, gold lay on the ground, ready to be picked up.

Some of them did find their golden dreams. Others lost everything they had and became workers for those who were luckier. Year after year, more of them came, as the search for gold went on.

In the beginning gold *was* easy to find in that fabulous section of California called El Dorado. It *could* be picked up from the ground or found gleaming in the streams. Those who arrived first staked out claims and guarded them day and night. Laws were forgotten. Men killed one another for a small piece of ground or a bag filled with yellow dust.

The late-comers had only the leavings, but sometimes they found that by digging they might strike a "vein" of the precious metal. Then they would follow that thin line of gold, digging deeper and deeper, until it disappeared into the earth. What all of them hoped to find was one huge piece of gold that would make them rich for life, and some of them succeeded. The largest gold nugget on record was found just beneath the earth's surface. It weighed 148 pounds. The lucky miner took it to San Francisco and sold it for $40,000. It would bring three times that much today. Other nuggets weighing 112, 96, and 72 pounds were found, plus many thousands that weighed only a few pounds each.

But where did those huge nuggets come from? The obvious answer was that somewhere in the area must be a vast storehouse of gold, a "mother lode." The early comers who had "worked out" their claims and the late arrivals began to search frantically for the immense nest of gold that lay beneath the ground.

Finally, ten years after Marshall picked up the first small nugget, a series of thick, rich veins of gold were discovered. They spread through almost seventy miles of an area on both sides of the American River. The mother lode had been found at last! The underground streams of yellow metal were the core of the California gold fields, but they were deep in the earth, and heavy equipment was needed to reach them.

Some miners combined their resources and formed companies. Others sold their claims to men who had come to California to find profitable investments. These "mining companies" began a systematic removal of the gold, and the headlong rush to find wealth came to an end.

Not only did the finding of the gold itself make some men rich, but many others, who had never handled a pick or shovel, became wealthy in other ways. Mining towns sprang up over night wherever a rich "strike" was made. These towns had dance halls, saloons, restaurants, and stores—anything and everything to ease the hard life of the miners. But every necessity and luxury was expensive. Eggs sold for $2 each. Flour was $10 a pound when it was available. An ordinary meal in a drab restaurant might cost $25. A bed in a bare room, occupied by a dozen other sleepers, could cost up to $50 a night. However, if a miner had a rich claim, he could afford the exorbitant prices. Every day some of them found nuggets and gold dust worth several thousands of dollars. Many others earned hundreds of dollars for every twenty-four hours of back-breaking labor. A large number of the gold-seekers found nothing at all and had to rob or beg for food.

Many of the mining towns had strange names: Poker Flat, Flea Town, Poverty Hill, Humbug Creek, Cut Eye, Hangtown, Lucky Creek, Piety Hill, Fair Play, and dozens of others. Almost all of these small towns have disappeared, or are lonely, uninhabited places in the desert where nothing moves but windblown tumbleweed, where wooden porches and railings sag and shutters slam against blank windows.

Nothing *alive* moves in those forgotten hamlets that saw so much violence, joy, and heartbreak.

But other things are there.

Strange events took place in those towns, events that cost people's lives and fortunes, so it must be true, as so many say who have visited those places, that the spirits of those whose lives reached a peak or sank into black despair there still haunt the dusty streets and abandoned wooden shacks.

Other mining towns survived, and are like nuggets on a chain of gold that stretches through the county of

El Dorado. And all of them have their ghosts. Downieville is one of them. Its ghost is the apparition of the only woman in California who was executed by hanging. She had killed her lover and was hung by her neck from a tree in the center of town for two days before she was cut down. The "hanging" tree was destroyed many years ago, but other trees are still standing there, and often a woman is seen wandering among them. Hair hangs over her face, and her head seems to be twisted on her neck.

Grass Valley is also on the golden chain. It is a city now, but when it was a village the famous dancer, Lola Montez, retired there after a lifetime of entertaining royalty all over the world. And there she died, penniless and forgotten by those who flattered her when she was young and beautiful. Her ghost often walks the streets in the old part of town, and it runs away with a youthful dancer's grace when anyone tries to speak to it.

Auburn, too, remains, and two ghosts trot their horses through its streets. Both were highwaymen. Tom Bell was the first man in the area to think it would be easier to hold up the stagecoaches carrying gold to the banks in San Francisco than to dig it out of the ground. But he was an unlucky bandit. Most of the stages he held up were not carrying gold. When he did happen to stop the right one he was shot dead on the spot by a guard.

Rattlesnake Dick was unlucky, too. He always got the blame when something was stolen, even though he was innocent. Finally he decided to give himself the name of Rattlesnake Dick and become a badman. He robbed stages for six years before a guard killed him. Both men are seen on the streets of the old part of town, sometimes together, sometimes alone, but they are cowardly ghosts, spurring their horses into a gallop and disappearing when people get close to them.

Placerville also has its ghost. His name is Snowshoe Thompson, and there are many tales about his great strength. He was a giant of a man, over seven feet tall and weighing more than 300 pounds. His job was to carry mail and supplies over the snow-covered mountains from Placerville to Carson City. One time, so they say, he made the journey with a full-size iron stove on his back. Even now when heavy things have to be moved, people will say, "Let's get Snowshoe Thompson to do it." They say it as a joke, and almost always it is, but there have been times in Placerville when very heavy objects seem to have moved themselves.

No other county in the United States saw so much turmoil, disorder, robbery, and murder in so short a time as did El Dorado, the golden heart of California. It is only natural that in that small area there are more ghosts and phantoms than any other place in the world.

But what of Sutter and Marshall, the two men who started it all? Where are their ghosts? And where, what, and whom do they haunt?

Sutter's apprehension came true. With the discovery of that first gold nugget, his empire came crashing down. His workers joined the rush for wealth, leaving his crops to rot in the fields. His cattle were stolen and were eaten by miners around roaring campfires. His mills, stores, and granaries stood empty. He even lost his land. The rush for gold and the greed of those who searched for it pushed him aside. Adventurers staked out claims on the land he had cultivated and left him to watch while they dug up fortunes from his fields. His wealth disappeared almost over night. At last, even though he had come to hate the word "gold" and what it had done to him, he began to search for it himself. But by that time the best places were guarded by men who would rather kill than give him a share, and the little he found was barely enough for food.

His love for California turned to hate. With a small wagon, some supplies, and two horses, he started the long journey back to the East. He settled in a small town in Pennsylvania, and there he spent the last few years of his life, a brokenhearted, penniless man who once had an empire. If there is one ghost that should haunt El Dorado county it is Sutter's. But no one has ever claimed to see it.

Marshall never left California. He didn't search for gold; he believed that because he had found the first nugget, *all* the gold was his. The spirits he talked with in his strange world told him all he need do was demand his share. He went from one mining camp to another, ordering the miners to give him gold. Some gave him food and bits of clothing, because he had no money and wore only rags. His tall, gaunt figure would appear suddenly at campfires or on the dusty streets of mining towns. He seemed to be everywhere at once, demanding that those who had benefited from his find should pay him for the discovery. He became a legend and a "character" to laugh at. Finally, after wandering for twenty-two years in the gold fields, he settled as a weary old man in the small town of Coloma, near the site of the sawmill he had started to build so long ago.

By then California had become the thirty-first state

to enter the Union, and the legend of James Marshall touched the hearts of some of the legislators in Sacramento, so the man who had found the first nugget, which led to millions of dollars in gold, was given a pension of $100 a month for life. He lived for thirteen more years, barely existing on his pension and on small gifts tourists gave him as he sat rocking on the porch of his small house.

Until the day he died he was convinced that all the gold in California belonged to him. But he was content to wait, he told the visitors who came to stare at the tall old man who had started the great gold rush of '49, because, he would add, his "spirits" had promised he would have revenge on those who had stolen his gold. When rumbling earthquakes shook the land, even then, he would nod and say, "The time is coming. The time is coming."

When he died his only request was to be buried on the spot where he had picked up what he thought was only a yellow stone. That area is now a state park, and the mill he almost finished building for John Sutter is being restored to what it was on that day when Marshall noticed the gleam in the water.

That place has one ghost that is more important than all the thousands of other phantoms that are crowded into the golden county of El Dorado. This ghost is tall and ragged and talks to spirits only he can see, as he walks along the banks of the water that flows through a millrace from the American River. This ghost never raises his eyes but stares steadily into the flowing stream.

Only he can see what others failed to see until he passed that way.

Index

114